Literacy by Design™

Writing Resource Guide

Rigby®
A Harcourt Achieve Imprint

www.Rigby.com
1-800-531-5015

Contents

GRAMMAR LESSONS

Theme 1

Theme 2

Theme 3

Theme 4

Theme 5

Theme 6

Theme 7

Theme 8

Theme 9

Theme 10

Theme 11

Theme 12

Theme 13

Theme 14

Theme 15

Theme 16

WRITING ORGANIZERS

WRITER'S CRAFT LESSONS

Using the Grammar Lessons and the Writer's Handbook

Grammar is an essential element in effective writing. Without this fundamental knowledge, students cannot convey their message to an audience.

Lesson Background
- Provides an explanation of the grammar skill.

Teaching the Lesson
- Direct, explicit instruction on the conventions that need to be mastered.

- Refers to the Writer's Handbook for definitions, examples, and grammar rules.

Extending the Lesson
- Reinforces and applies the strategies and techniques targeted during Teaching the Lesson.

On Your Own
- Provides students with an opportunity to practice the skill on their own or with partners.

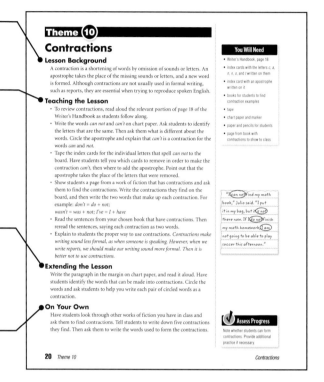

Using the Writer's Handbook
The Writer's Handbook is a valuable reference book for both teachers and students. It can be used with the grammar focus lessons in this guide or to introduce grade-level grammar skills. As students become familiar with grammar, they can use this book as a reference to answer questions about spelling, capitalization, grammar, and usage.

The Writer's Handbook is:

- For teachers to use as they teach focus lessons on grammar, usage, and mechanics during writing instruction.

- For students to use during the Writing Workshop.

Using the Writing Organizers

The Writing Organizers are reproducible graphic organizers that students use, first in groups and then individually, to develop concepts during prewriting. They are a basic framework for students' compositions. Before students use the Writing Organizers, they have participated in the shared writing process with a teacher using the Writing Transparencies. The Writing Organizer duplicates the graphic organizer used on the Writing Transparency.

Each Writing Workshop focuses on an organizational pattern or a writing form. When featured in explicit instruction, writing forms act as an important supportive frame in which students compose their own ideas. The Writing Organizers provide a hands-on, visual framework to help students organize their ideas and plan their writing.

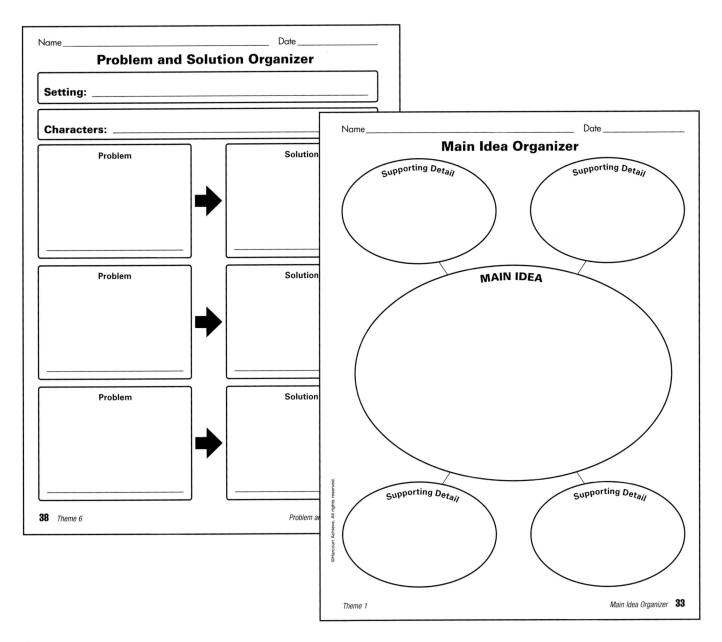

Using the Writer's Craft Lessons

Daily attention to writer's craft – which covers a host of tools and topics – is an essential way to improve students' writing while reinforcing the notion that the writing process is a craft.

Lesson Background
- Defines the Writer's Craft strategy.

Teaching the Lesson
- Focuses on selections (on the blackline master) that provide a model of the strategy to be addressed in the lesson.

- Guided instruction allows students to analyze and practice the targeted skill in a whole group setting.

Extending the Lesson
- Reinforces skills, strategies, and techniques in small groups or independent writing.

- Focuses on applying the craft skill to students' own work.

On Your Own
- Provides practice in the skill individually or with a partner.

- Encourages the use of the Writer's Notebook.

Whole Group Activity
- Provides a text and an activity for students to practice the craft skill.

- The blackline master can be copied or made into a transparency for instruction.

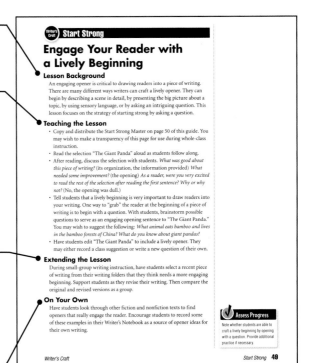

Writing Assessment Rubric

The *Literacy by Design* Writing Assessment Rubric contains key behavioral indicators for holistically evaluating the development of young writers. Use the rubric not only to identify the developmental stage of your students but also to plot their future growth, both within and across stages. (See the Writing Assessment Rubric Form on page xi.)

	Experimenting Stage	Emerging Stage
Content Ideas and Organization	• Scribbles emulate the look of writing; some may carry meaning. • Simple illustrations represent ideas. • Student shares ideas orally; ideas may lack focus and may vary upon subsequent retellings. • Student may attempt organization by grouping scribbles or illustrations together.	• Illustrations begin to have more detail. • Student orally explains ideas and may elaborate on illustrations or written words and phrases. • Some ideas begin to take shape, but a clear message or storyline may not be present. • Organization continues to develop as student groups similar words and illustrations. • With prompting, student can state audience and purpose.
Language Sentence Fluency, Word Choice, and Voice	• Student shows an awareness that illustrations and written words are different. • Student knows letters and begins to experiment with sound-letter relationships, although some letters may be random. • Illustrations represent common words and generally lack distinguishing features.	• Student demonstrates understanding of one-to-one correspondence between written and spoken words (e.g., student points while reading). • Writing takes the form of simple, common words, phrases, or sentences. • Voice begins to emerge as student adds personal touches to writing and illustrations.
Mechanics Writing Conventions	• Student begins to show an awareness of left-right writing directionality. • Student writes strings of letters and may begin to group letters into words, whether pretend or actual. • Writing is not always legible.	• Clear words emerge, with proper spacing. • Student experiments with uppercase and lowercase letters. • Student begins to group words together into phrases and sentences, arranging them from left to right. • A number of words may be spelled phonetically.
Process Writing Purpose, Process, and Presentation	• Student relies on teacher prompting to draw or "write" about a specific idea. • Student talks about (or explains) work and can be prompted to add to it (e.g., can add more details to a drawing). • Final work may be scattered and disordered on page; illustrations may be labeled.	• Student understands the purpose of and relies upon a small number of text forms (e.g., story, letter). • With guidance, student talks to generate ideas for writing. • Student draws pictures or writes words/phrases about a specific idea. • Student can be prompted to add to the work and make simple corrections. • Final work is mostly legible and more organized; clear use of simple fiction and nonfiction text features (e.g., labels, titles) emerges.

Developing Stage	Proficient Stage	Advanced Stage
• Illustrations, if present, begin to support writing rather than substitute for writing. • A message or storyline is present but may lack a clear beginning or a clear ending. • Some ideas are supported with details but may lack focus. • Ideas show a more formal attempt at organization; some sequencing and use of simple transitions (e.g., words such as *next* or *then*) may be present.	• A clear message or storyline is present, with a serviceable beginning and ending. • Ideas are focused and supported with sufficient details; some details may be weak or off topic. • Ideas are generally well organized; student begins to use more complex transitions to achieve greater passage-level coherence (e.g., transitions that link key content and ideas from sentence to sentence). • Student begins to make choices about ideas and organization to suit audience and purpose.	• A clear message or storyline is present, with an engaging beginning and ending. • Ideas are focused and fully supported with strong, relevant details. • Ideas are well organized; use of transitions and other devices results in writing that is smooth, coherent, and easy to follow. • Student makes strong, effective choices about ideas and organization to suit audience and purpose.
• Simple and compound sentences are used in writing. • Student begins to experiment with different sentence types and syntactical patterns that aid fluency, but overall writing may still be choppy. • Student correctly uses and relies upon a small bank of mostly common words; student may begin to experiment with less common words. • More frequent hints of voice and personality are present, but writing continues to be mostly mechanical.	• More fluent writing emerges through the use of an increasing variety of sentence types and syntactical patterns. • Student correctly uses a large bank of common words; student effectively experiments with new words and begins to choose words more purposefully (e.g., to create images or to have an emotional impact). • Voice continues to develop as student experiments with language.	• All sentence types are present. • Student writes fluently, varying sentence types, sentence beginnings, and grammatical structures. • Student uses an extensive bank of common and less common words correctly; student successfully uses words with precision and purpose. • Voice is expressive, engaging, and appropriate to audience and purpose.
• Sentences have beginning capitalization and ending punctuation; student experiments with other marks (e.g., commas). • Paragraphing begins to emerge. • Spelling is more conventional, especially for high frequency words. • Awareness of usage (i.e., that there are rules to be followed) begins to develop; student experiments with simple usage conventions, but success is variable.	• Student correctly uses all marks of end punctuation; correct use of some other marks is evident, especially in typical situations (e.g., a comma before the conjunction in a compound sentence or a colon to introduce a list). • Student correctly spells most high frequency words and begins to transfer spelling "rules" to lesser-known words. • Writing demonstrates basic understanding of standard grade-level grammar and usage.	• Student correctly and effectively uses standard grade-level punctuation, including more sophisticated marks and usages (e.g., dashes to emphasize key ideas). • Student correctly spells a wide variety of words, both common and uncommon. • Writing demonstrates full and effective control of standard grade-level grammar and usage; overall usage aids reading.
• Student experiments with a variety of text forms and begins to understand how purpose determines form. • Student generates limited prewriting ideas. • With teacher support, draft shows some development but continues to be mostly skeletal. • Student revisits the work but mostly to correct a few line-level errors (e.g., end punctuation and spelling). • Student begins to move more naturally and independently through the writing process. • Final work is generally neat; an increasing variety of fiction and nonfiction text features (e.g., titles, headings, charts, captions) is present, but features may be more for show than for support of message.	• Student demonstrates increasing control over a variety of text forms and can choose form to suit purpose. • Student generates sufficient prewriting ideas. • Draft shows good development of prewriting, including effective attempts at focusing, organizing, and elaborating ideas. • Student revisits the work not only to correct errors but also to address some passage-level issues (e.g., clarity of message, sufficiency of details); student may use supporting resources (e.g., dictionary, grammar book). • Sense that the process is purposeful begins to emerge. • Final work is neat; use of various fiction and nonfiction text features tends to support and clarify meaning.	• Student effectively controls a variety of text forms and can choose form to suit purpose. • Student uses prewriting ideas as a plan that is both general and flexible. • Draft shows strong development of prewriting and may effectively depart from prewriting as a signal of the student's overall writing maturity. • Student revisits the work not only to correct errors but also to address key passage-level issues. • Overall, student shows investment in the craft of writing and moves through the stages smoothly and recursively. • Final work is neat; effective use of fiction and nonfiction text features results in a polish that strengthens the student's overall message.

Snapshots of Young Writers

Writing samples, or anchor papers, provide powerful snapshots of writing development—snapshots key to understanding students' control over written language and to determining subsequent paths of instruction. The following writing samples represent each of the five stages of development in the *Literacy by Design* Writing Assessment Rubric. The samples for each stage are preceded by a brief summary of key behavioral indicators for that stage.

Experimenting Stage

- Writing is mostly an attempt to emulate adult writing.
- It includes single letters, letter strings, and simple illustrations.
- Writing attempts to be communicative, but most letters and letter strings do not carry consistent meaning.

Nour

Mireya

Emerging Stage

- Writing shows an understanding that spoken words can be written down and read by others.
- It includes the use of content-bearing words, phrases, and short sentences.
- Writing may demonstrate right-left directionality and experimentation with capital letters and end marks.
- It includes many words spelled phonetically.

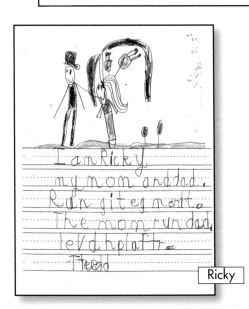

Ricky

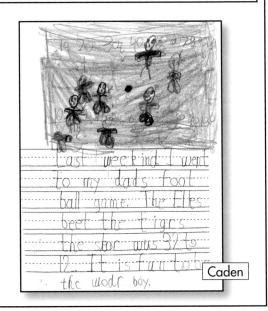

Caden

Developing Stage

- Writing exhibits growing control over writing conventions, including more conventional spelling, punctuation, and grammar.
- Writing carries a simple message supported by some details.
- Sentence structure is mostly formulaic and mechanical.
- It includes a limited number of text forms.

Dear Bob
I LiKe to play x Box Because
It has all the cool games on it.
I also like to ride my schott
becaus it runs so smothley.
I like to play conputt it has
a lot of games Like Rollrcost
tiy conra.

Sinsirly mason

Mason

Irric 9-19-06

football

On Saturday I have to play football.
I have to play the Lions. I am a
running back. I am really fast. I like
playing football. My favorite T.V. show
is football. It is fun to watch football.
My mom and dad like to watch football
too. We like to eat popcorn when we
are watchingr football.

Irric

Proficient Stage

- Writing includes a clear, focused message supported by sufficient details.
- It exhibits most grade-level conventions.
- Writing includes a variety of sentence structures.
- It shows a growing awareness of audience and purpose.
- It demonstrates control over a variety of text forms.

Texas and Alaska

Texas and Alaska have many differences and have a lot of similarities at the same time. I've lived in Texas all my life and I know Alaska is different. I have been fascinated about Alaska because of its differences.

Texas and Alaska are similar in these ways: They are both part of the U.S., they were both part of another country before they joined the U.S., and they both have the same amount senators.

Texas did a very important action, by sending a plane around the world non-stop. It took 94 hours and refueled 4 times while in flight. The plane was called Lucky Lady II. Alaska has a highway that stretches 1,422 miles between Dawson Creek and Anchorage.

Texas is not nearly as big as Alaska. Alaska is 1/3 the size of the U.S. Texas is only 737 miles east to west and 744 miles north to south. In Texas it rarely snows. In Alaska, however, it snows from late summer to late spring. Texas may have a lot of coast line, but Alaska has a little over 1000 miles of coast line while Texas only has 500 miles of coast line.

So, you learned about the similarities and differences between Alaska and Texas. I like Texas because Texas rarely goes below 36 degrees and the ocean water is always warm and Texas has a lot of historical monuments. I would not be able to live in Alaska because it is cold and in the summer it is always light all the time and in winter it is dark.

Nick

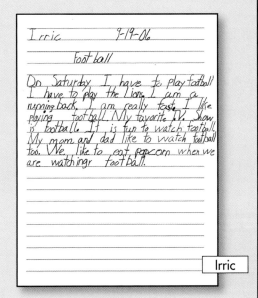

The Perrrfect Birthday

How fun was one of your
birthdays? Well all of my birthdays
Were pretty fun, but I'm going to tell
you about my 8th birthday.

It was my 8th birthday
when I woke up to a place that
was very unusual. This place was
my regular home? I said to my
self, but what was different?
After 5 minutes I figured it
out. My Mom had signs that
said "Happy Birthday!", Hey 8 year
old and one was a poem that my
mom had worked really hard on.
I was really Surprised. When
I got down stairs my mom said,
"Happy Birthday!"
The time came when my friends
everybody came for my party. Justin
Jessica Gus and Prethi were ready
to Swim. The party
My theme was under the
ocean, like the Arica Speaking of Ariel
I dressed up like her.

Chandni

Advanced Stage

- Writing demonstrates mastery of conventions and purposeful variety of sentence structures.
- It includes a strong, focused message that is fully supported and engaging in presentation.
- Writing exhibits a clear understanding of audience and purpose.
- It shows effective use of word choice, voice, details, and text form.

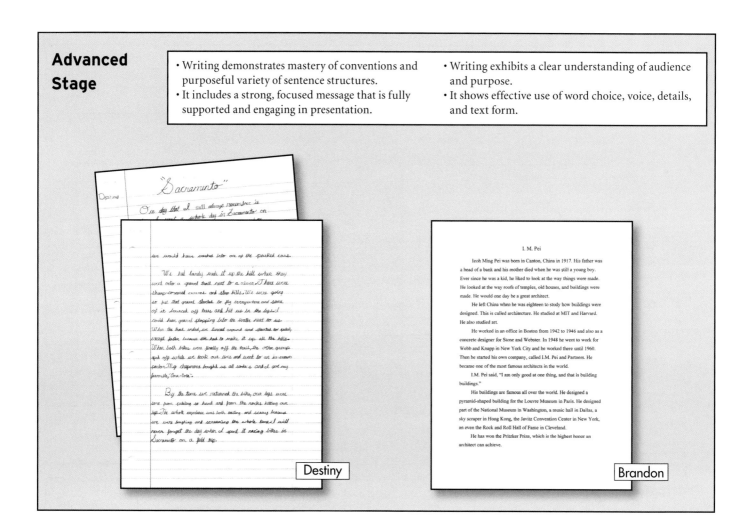

Destiny

Brandon

Writing Stages According to Grade Level

	Experimenting Stage	Emerging Stage	Developing Stage	Proficient Stage	Advanced Stage
Grade K	██████████				
Grade 1		████████████			
Grade 2			████████████		
Grade 3				████████	
Grade 4				████████████	
Grade 5				████████████	

Writing Assessment Rubric Form

Student's Name _____ **Date** _____

(1) • Based on an initial review of a representative sampling of student work, identify the student's most likely stage of development. Locate that stage on the rubric and then review the behavioral indicators for each of the four instructional categories: Content, Language, Mechanics, and Process.
• If the indicators for a particular category mostly describe the student's work, check the appropriate box.
• The student is considered to be in a particular stage if at least three category boxes in that stage have been checked. If fewer than three boxes are checked, the student is considered to be in the previous stage.

	Experimenting	Emerging	Developing	Proficient	Advanced
Content Ideas and Organization	☐	☐	☐	☐	☐
Language Sentence Fluency, Word Choice, and Voice	☐	☐	☐	☐	☐
Mechanics Writing Conventions	☐	☐	☐	☐	☐
Process Writing Purpose, Process, and Presentation	☐	☐	☐	☐	☐

Stage _____

(2) • Note observations about key strengths and weaknesses.
• Tie observations to specific strategies to be used in future instruction.

Observations	Notes for Future Instruction
Strengths	
Growth Areas	

* It is recommended that you use the *Literacy by Design* Writing Assessment Rubric to evaluate a sampling of each student's writing at least three times a year.

Managing Writing Workshop

Independent Writing at the Core

Similar to reading workshop, writing workshop is the time when a teacher works with a small group of students to differentiate writing instruction. Other students are engaged in writing independently, whether that means generating ideas, writing a draft, or revising their writing.

Students learn to write with practice. They need ample classroom time to explore ideas and refine their writing skills. Independent writing allows students to apply the strategies and skills they are learning in whole class and small group instruction.

A key difference between small group writing and small group reading is that student writers are typically working on the same piece as they move from the group to independent work. In fact, a writer might continue work on the same writing piece over several small group sessions, continuing to work on the piece between sessions in independent writing as well. Having the two activities occur simultaneously in the same workshop emphasizes the connection between small group and independent writing.

Making Independent Writing Successful

- **Conference regularly with writers**. Meet with students to ensure they use their Writer's Notebook or other resources when recording ideas and finding writing topics (See *Comprehensive Teacher's Guide*, Writing Conference Form, page A23).

- **Provide a focus for independent writing**. Choose a writing form, organizational pattern, process, or trait that is taught in the theme to serve as a focus for students during independent writing.

- **Offer prompts when writers get stuck**. The best source for writing ideas is a student's Writer's Notebook, but occasionally students just get stuck. Provide specific prompts related to the theme's instructional focus that can be used when students are having difficulty identifying a topic for their writing.

Setting Up Writing Workshop

In a successful writing workshop, students understand and embrace the opportunity to explore ideas and mold those ideas into text. Planning requires setting up materials and creating an environment in which students can manage their independent writing time effectively.

Create a Space for a Successful Writing Workshop

- Designated place for students to keep their **writing folders** and **Writer's Notebooks**

- **Reference area** with dictionaries, encyclopedias, and thesauruses

- **Writing center** with magazines and other visual materials to spark ideas

- Wall space to display **shared** and **interactive writing pieces**

- Copies of **graphic organizers** to capture and organize writing ideas (see pages 33–48)

Simple and Compound Sentences

Lesson Background

A simple sentence has a single independent clause. It contains a subject and a predicate. The predicate may have a single verb or a verb group. A compound sentence is made of two independent clauses. The clauses are usually joined by a conjunction, such as *and*, *but*, or *so* and a comma.

Teaching the Lesson

- To review simple and compound sentences, read aloud the relevant portion of page 35 of the Writer's Handbook as students follow along.
- Write the following sentence on chart paper: *The farmer chased his cows.* Ask students to identify the subject and the predicate. Explain that a simple sentence has one subject and one predicate.
- Replace the period from the sentence on the chart paper with a comma. Then write *and then he herded them into the barn* and add a period. Ask students to identify the subject and predicate in the new sentence. Explain that a compound sentence is two simple sentences put together with a connecting word, such as *and*, *but*, or *so*. Remind students that a comma goes after the first sentence.
- Tape the sentence and connecting word strips to the board. Punctuate the sentences. Have students tell you which strips to move to create new compound sentences. Change the punctuation and capitalization to reflect the sentence structure changes. Read the compound sentences aloud.
- Explain to students the proper formation of simple and compound sentences. *Simple sentences contain one subject and one predicate. Compound sentences are two simple sentences put together with a connecting word, such as* and, but, *or* so. *A comma is inserted after the first sentence.*

Extending the Lesson

Write the paragraph in the margin on chart paper and read it aloud. Have students identify the simple and compound sentences. Ask volunteers to draw circles around the simple sentences and underline the compound sentences.

On Your Own

Divide students into groups. Have each group write a paragraph about what they might see on a farm. Ask them to use two compound sentences and two simple sentences. Have them draw a circle around the simple sentences and underline the compound sentences.

You Will Need

- Writer's Handbook, page 35
- sentence strips with the following sentences written on them:
  The farmer fed the cows
  The cows fell asleep
  The farmer's wife picked apples
  The tree still had many apples
  The farmer's son knocked over the milk pail
  The milk spilled
- tape
- chart paper and marker
- paper and pencils for each group
- word strips with the following words written on them: *and, so, but*

> The Franklin family raises many animals on its farm.
> Ducks swim in the pond, and cows graze in the field.
> Dogs run in the backyard, and cats sleep in the barn.
> The Franklin family loves animals.

✔ Assess Progress

Note whether students are able to correctly identify simple and compound sentences. Provide additional practice if necessary.

Simple and Compound Subjects/Predicates

Lesson Background

A simple subject has only one part, while a compound subject has two or more parts joined by *and*. A simple predicate has only one part, while a compound predicate has two or more parts joined by a connecting word, such as *and*, *or*, or *but*.

Teaching the Lesson

- To review simple and compound subjects and predicates, read aloud the relevant portion of page 34 of the Writer's Handbook as students follow along.
- Write the following sentence on chart paper: *Myra and Lee visited the museum and walked by the park.* Ask students to identify the subjects. Circle *Myra* and *Lee*. Explain that this sentence has two subjects joined by the connecting word *and*. Tell them that this is called a compound subject. Next ask students to identify the predicates. Underline *visited the museum* and *walked by the park*. Explain that the sentence has a compound predicate: two predicates joined by a connecting word.
- Tape one sentence strip to the board and ask students to identify whether it has a simple or compound subject. Then ask whether it has a simple or compound predicate. Ask them to explain their reasoning. Repeat with the remaining sentence strips.
- Explain to students the forms of simple and compound subjects and predicates. *Simple subjects and predicates have one part. Compound subjects and predicates have two or more parts joined by a connecting word.*

Extending the Lesson

Write the paragraph in the margin on chart paper and read it aloud. Have students identify the subjects and circle them. Tell them to write *simple* above simple subjects and *compound* above compound subjects. Have them identify, underline, and label the simple and compound predicates.

On Your Own

Have students look through books you have in class to find and write down one example of each of the following: a simple subject, a simple predicate, a compound subject, and a compound predicate.

Myra and Lee brought their lunches. Myra ate a sandwich and drank some juice. Lee ate a salad. Then Myra and Lee went back into the museum. Myra wanted to see the dinosaur exhibit. Lee didn't want to see dinosaurs but wanted to see airplanes.

Assess Progress

Note whether students understand simple and compound subjects and predicates. Provide additional practice if necessary.

Subject-Verb Agreement

Lesson Background

The subject of a sentence must agree with the verb in the sentence. When using a singular subject, use a singular verb. When using a plural subject, use a plural verb. Subject-verb agreement is essential for conveying meaning.

Teaching the Lesson

- To review subject-verb agreement, read aloud the relevant portion of page 24 of the Writer's Handbook as students follow along.
- Write the following sentence on chart paper: *Sarita wants a new bike.* Point out that *Sarita* is a singular subject (she is only one person) and *wants* is a singular verb (it is used for one person). Then write *The bikes gleam in the sun.* Point out that *bikes* is a plural subject (there is more than one bike) and *gleam* is a plural verb (it is used for more than one thing).
- Draw a T-chart on the board. Label the left column *Subjects* and the right column *Verbs*. Tape the index cards in random order next to the chart. Have students identify which words are subjects and which are verbs. Then move the cards to the correct columns. Invite students to match subjects to verbs so they agree. Tell students that they should read the combinations quietly to themselves to confirm that their subjects and verbs agree.
- Explain to students the proper ways to create subject-verb agreement in their sentences. *When using a singular subject, use a singular verb. When using a plural subject, use a plural verb.*

Extending the Lesson

Write the paragraph in the margin on chart paper and read it aloud. Have students circle the verbs that need to be changed so that the verbs agree with the subjects. Write in the correct verbs. (pick, rides, is, ride, doesn't)

On Your Own

Divide the class into pairs. Have one student from each pair look through books to find two sentences with singular subjects and verbs. Ask the student's partner to look through books to find two sentences with plural subjects and verbs. Have them exchange papers and check each other's work.

You Will Need

- Writer's Handbook, page 24
- index cards with the subjects *dog, cow, cat, goose, dogs, cows, cats, geese* written on them; and cards with the verbs *runs, flies, naps, eats, honk, bark, meow, moo* written on them
- tape
- chart paper and marker
- books for agreement examples
- paper and pencils for students

> Alexi and his mother (picks) a red bike for the boy. He (ride) it through the neighborhood. The bike (are) fast and shiny. Alexi and his mom (rides) together sometimes. Alexi (don't) ride very far on his own.

Assess Progress

Note whether students understand subject-verb agreement. Provide additional practice if necessary.

Review Sentence Structure

Lesson Background

Simple sentences have one independent clause. Compound sentences contain two simple sentences joined by a conjunction and a comma. Simple subjects have one noun that performs the action of the sentence, while compound subjects have more than one. Simple predicates contain one verb, while compound predicates contain more than one.

Teaching the Lesson

- To review sentence structure, read aloud the relevant portions of pages 34–35 of the Writer's Handbook as students follow along.
- Write the following sentence on chart paper: *Theresa and André ran to school.* Ask students to identify the subject. Point out that *Theresa and André* is a compound subject because it has two nouns. Ask students to identify the predicate. Point out that *ran to school* is a simple predicate because only one action is being performed.
- Write the following sentence on chart paper: *Theresa ran to school and walked into the classroom.* Ask students what has changed about the sentence. Note the simple subject and compound predicate.
- Write the following sentence on chart paper: *Theresa likes to climb trees, but André likes to draw.* Ask students if the sentence could be split into two sentences. Remind them that two simple sentences joined by a connecting word, such as *but*, and a comma make a compound sentence.
- Explain to students the various structures of sentences. *Simple subjects have one noun, and compound subjects have more than one noun. Simple predicates contain one action, and compound predicates include more than one action. Simple sentences express one complete thought. Compound sentences contain two simple sentences joined by a connecting word, such as* and, but, *or* so.

Extending the Lesson

Write the sentences in the margin on chart paper. Have students copy them and decide whether each sentence has a simple or compound subject and a simple or compound predicate.

On Your Own

Divide the class into groups of four. Have each group find two examples of simple sentences and compound sentences in books you have in the classroom. Have groups exchange papers and check one another's work.

You Will Need

- Writer's Handbook, pages 34–35
- chart paper and marker
- books for sentence examples
- paper and pencils for groups and individual students

1. Singh and Erin like to play kickball. [compound subject, simple predicate]
2. The ball bounces across the field and lands next to the fence. [simple subject, compound predicate]
3. Erin catches the big red ball. [simple subject, simple predicate]
4. Erin and Singh score runs and win games. [compound subject, compound predicate]

Assess Progress

Note whether students are able to form sentences correctly. Provide additional practice if necessary.

Theme ③

Declarative/Interrogative Sentences

Lesson Background

A declarative sentence states a fact or an idea and ends in a period. An interrogative sentence asks a question and ends in a question mark. An interrogative sentence is a direct question that requires an answer.

Teaching the Lesson

- To review declarative and interrogative sentences, read aloud the relevant portion of page 35 of the Writer's Handbook as students follow along.
- Tell students to listen as you read aloud. *Animals need our help to protect them. What can you do to help protect animals in your community?* Write both sentences on chart paper. Tell students that the first sentence is a declarative sentence, meaning it tells facts or ideas. Point out the period to students and write *Declarative Sentence* next to the sentence. Tell them that the second sentence is an interrogative sentence, meaning it asks a question. Point out the question mark to students and write *Interrogative Sentence* next to the question.
- Divide students into groups of four. Have each group look at a book or magazine and pick out two examples of declarative sentences (statements) and two examples of interrogative sentences (questions).
- Have each group share one declarative sentence and one interrogative sentence with the class. Ask students how they knew which sentences were declarative and which were interrogative.
- Explain to students the difference between declarative and interrogative sentences. *Declarative sentences state a fact or an idea and end with a period. Interrogative sentences ask a question and end with a question mark.*

Extending the Lesson

Divide students into pairs. Tell them that they must find out their partner's favorite sport, animal, and song. They will need to write down three questions to ask their partner. Have them record their partner's responses in complete sentences.

On Your Own

Have students write a paragraph about their favorite book. Tell them to use at least three declarative sentences and one interrogative sentence.

You Will Need

- Writer's Handbook, page 35
- chart paper and marker
- books or magazines for examples
- paper and pencils for pairs and individual students

Assess Progress

Note whether students can differentiate between declarative and interrogative sentences. Provide additional practice if necessary.

Theme **3**

Imperative/Exclamatory Sentences

Lesson Background

An imperative sentence orders someone to do something. It ends with either a period or an exclamation point, depending on the forcefulness of the order. An exclamatory sentence is a more powerful version of a declarative sentence. It shows strong emotion, such as surprise, joy, or anger, and ends with an exclamation point.

Teaching the Lesson

- To review imperative and exclamatory sentences, read aloud the relevant portion of page 36 of the Writer's Handbook as students follow along.
- Tell students to listen as you read aloud: *My hamster escaped from its cage! Help me find it.* Write the two sentences on chart paper. Tell students that the first sentence is an exclamatory sentence. Write *Exclamatory Sentence* on the chart paper. Point out the exclamation point and discuss how the sentence shows strong emotion. Explain that the second sentence is an imperative sentence. Write *Imperative Sentence* on chart paper. Point out the period and discuss how the sentence gives a command.
- Write the following sentences on chart paper: *We won the game! Clean up your mess! That painting is beautiful!* Ask students which sentences are imperative and which are exclamatory. Ask them to explain their reasoning.
- Explain that the second sentence is imperative because it demands that the reader do something (clean up the mess). Tell students that the first and last sentences are exclamatory. They both state a fact or an idea and show excitement.
- Explain to students the difference between imperative and exclamatory sentences. *Imperative sentences command someone to do something. Exclamatory sentences state a fact or an idea and show strong emotion.*

Extending the Lesson

Divide the students into groups of four. Write the list of sentences in the margin on chart paper. Have each group decide which sentences are exclamatory and which are imperative. Go over the correct answers with each group.

On Your Own

Have each group write a paragraph about someone being surprised. Tell them to include at least one exclamatory sentence and one imperative sentence.

You Will Need

- Writer's Handbook, page 36
- chart paper and marker
- paper and pencils for each group

1. The dog ran away!
   [exclamatory]
2. Open your book to the first page. [imperative]
3. Give me a paper towel! [imperative]
4. Thank you so much! [exclamatory]

 Assess Progress

Note whether students can differentiate between imperative and exclamatory sentences. Provide additional practice if necessary.

Sentence Combining

Lesson Background

Consecutive sentences that either repeat subjects or repeat predicates can be merged into sentences with compound subjects or compound predicates. Sentence combining improves the flow of writing.

Teaching the Lesson

- To review sentence combining, read aloud the relevant portions of pages 34–35 of the Writer's Handbook as students follow along.
- Write the following sentences on chart paper: *Keisha got her backpack. Ken got his backpack. Samir got his backpack.* Read them aloud. Ask students to identify a problem with this group of sentences. Explain that when sentences have a similar structure, they can be combined. Write the combined sentence: *Keisha, Ken, and Samir got their backpacks.* Point out that in this case, the subjects are combined.
- Write the following sentences on chart paper: *The cat got up. The cat stretched. The cat licked its paws.* Read the sentences aloud. Ask students to identify a problem with this group of sentences. Explain that the predicates of these sentences can be combined. Write the combined sentence on chart paper: *The cat got up, stretched, and licked its paws.*
- Explain to students one way to combine sentences. *If two or more sentences are about the same subject or have the same predicate, combine the sentences to make one longer sentence that does not repeat itself.*

Extending the Lesson

Write the sentences in the margin on chart paper. Have students determine which sentences have similar subjects and which have similar predicates. Then have them try to combine the sentences. Write the resulting combined sentences on the chart paper.

On Your Own

Have students write a brief paragraph about an activity they enjoy. Have students trade papers and combine sentences that have a similar structure. Tell students to make edits on the page and return it to the writer.

You Will Need

- Writer's Handbook, pages 34–35
- chart paper and marker
- paper and pencils for students

1. Sitha went to Yellowstone Park. Sitha also went to Canada.

2. Marcos had a birthday in September. Khalid had a birthday in September.

3. The fans watched the basketball player dribble. Then the fans watched her shoot the ball.

4. So Mai rode a horse. Her friend Marie rode a horse.

 Assess Progress

Note whether students understand when and how to combine sentences. Monitor progress in their writing.

Theme ④

Review Sentence Combining

Lesson Background

The previous lesson stressed the following point: Consecutive sentences that repeat either subjects or predicates can be merged into sentences with compound subjects or compound predicates. Sentence combining improves the flow of writing.

Teaching the Lesson

- To review sentence combining, read aloud the relevant portions of pages 34–35 of the Writer's Handbook as students follow along.
- Remind students that if two or more sentences have a similar structure or are about the same subject, they can combine the sentences to make one longer sentence.
- Write the paragraph in the margin on chart paper and ask students which sentences can be combined. Based on their suggestions, rewrite the paragraph.
- Explain to students when to combine sentences. *If sentences have similar subjects or similar predicates, you can combine them to make longer sentences that don't repeat information.*

Extending the Lesson

Ask students to write *I like to eat _____.* on a sheet of paper three different times. Tell them to fill in the three blanks with names of their favorite foods. Then ask them to combine the three sentences into one new sentence. Volunteers can read their new sentences aloud. Then ask the class, *Who wrote down "pizza" as a favorite food?* Record those names on the chart paper. Write a new sentence: *_____, _____, and _____ like to eat pizza.* Insert students' names in the blanks.

On Your Own

Have each student look at a composition he or she wrote recently. Instruct students to rewrite their compositions, combining any repetitive groups of sentences they find.

You Will Need

- Writer's Handbook, pages 34–35
- chart paper and marker
- recent compositions students have written, one per student
- paper and pencils for students

Henri got a ticket for the school play. Lisa got a ticket for the school play. Henri and Lisa were excited when the curtain opened. Henri and Lisa thought the music was beautiful. The lead actress remembered all of her lines. The lead actor remembered all of his lines. Henri and Lisa enjoyed the show.

Assess Progress

Note whether students understand when and how to combine sentences. Monitor progress as students revise their written work in class.

Common and Proper Nouns

Lesson Background

Nouns name people, places, things, or ideas. Common nouns name nonspecific people, places, things, or ideas. Proper nouns begin with a capital letter and name specific people, places, and things.

Teaching the Lesson

- To review common and proper nouns, read aloud the relevant portion of page 20 of the Writer's Handbook as students follow along.
- Draw a T-chart on chart paper. Title the left side *Common Nouns* and the right side *Proper Nouns*. Have students volunteer names of their favorite foods. Write the first two responses next to the chart. Repeat with students' favorite character in a book, favorite animal, and favorite movie. Ask students to decide which answers are common nouns and which are proper nouns. Rewrite the words in the correct column. Point out that the proper nouns are capitalized and the common nouns are not capitalized.
- Explain to students the difference between common and proper nouns. *A common noun names a general person, place, thing, or idea. A proper noun names a specific person, place, or thing.*

Extending the Lesson

Write the sentences in the margin on chart paper. Have students identify the common noun and the proper noun in each sentence. Have students determine which words should be capitalized. Replace the lowercase letters with capital letters as appropriate.

On Your Own

Give each student an index card with a common noun written on it. Have students write as many proper nouns as they can for the common noun on the card. When they finish, have them trade cards with another student. Then have students try to add three more proper nouns to the new card.

You Will Need

- Writer's Handbook, page 20
- chart paper and marker
- enough index cards for each student to have one; each will have one of the following common nouns written on it: *author, book, cartoon character, city, country, holiday, school, sports team, state, teacher*
- pencils for students

---

1. My brother visited jane.
[brother = common, Jane = proper]
2. Los angeles is a big city.
[Los Angeles = proper, city = common]
3. The second planet is venus.
[planet = common, Venus = proper]
4. Her puppy is named ollie.
[puppy = common, Ollie = proper]

Assess Progress

Note whether students are able to differentiate between common and proper nouns. Reinforce understanding as the class reads other material with common and proper nouns.

Theme ⑤
Singular and Plural Nouns

Lesson Background

Students already know nouns as naming words. Singular nouns name only one person, place, thing, or idea. Plural nouns name a set of people, places, things, or ideas. While most nouns can be made plural by simply adding an -*s*, other nouns require -*es*, -*ies*, or another alternative in order to be made plural.

Teaching the Lesson

- To review singular and plural nouns, read aloud the relevant portion of page 20 of the Writer's Handbook as students follow along.
- Write these four words on chart paper: *house, triangle, chicken, flower.* Ask students to make each word plural. Write the plural forms next to the singular forms on the chart paper.
- Review these rules for plurals:

   In general, add an -*s* to the end of the word.

   Words that end in -*sh*, -*ch*, -*ss*, or -*x* require an -*es*.

   If there is a consonant plus a -*y* at the end of a word, change the -*y* to *i* and add -*es* in the plural form.

- Choose two nouns that require -*es* (e.g., *watch, box*). Have students state the singular and plural. Write both forms of the word on chart paper. Point out the -*es*, and note that you can hear the extra syllable in words that end in -*es*. Choose two nouns that end in -*y* (e.g., *donkey, daisy*). Have students state the singular and plural. Write both forms of the words on the chart paper, and note the change in spelling (*donkeys, daisies*). Point out that words that end in -*ey* get just an -*s*, but most words that end in -*y* change to -*ies*.
- Explain to students the proper way to form plurals. *You form plural nouns by adding an -s or an -es to a word. Words that end in -ey in the singular form get just an -s in the plural form. Most words that end in -y in the singular form end in -ies in the plural form.*

Extending the Lesson

Divide students into groups of four. Have each group write down the singular and plural forms of the ten nouns in the margin as you dictate them. Go over the correct answers with each group.

On Your Own

Have students make a list of ten items in the classroom. Tell them to write the singular form if the classroom has only one of an item, or the plural form if the classroom has more than one of the item.

door (doors)
patch (patches)
baby (babies)
dish (dishes)
pony (ponies)
picture (pictures)
wish (wishes)
turkey (turkeys)
lunch (lunches)
fox (foxes)

 **Assess Progress**

Note whether students are able to differentiate between singular and plural nouns. Provide additional practice if necessary.

Possessive Nouns

Lesson Background

A possessive noun is a noun that possesses, or owns, another noun. The addition of an apostrophe and the letter -*s* shows possession of one noun by another. Plural possessives that end in -*s* are simply followed by an apostrophe.

Teaching the Lesson

- To review possessive nouns, read aloud the relevant portions of pages 19 and 21 of the Writer's Handbook as students follow along.
- Write *Gina* and *pen* on chart paper. Tell students that Gina owns the pen. Ask them how to show this. Add an apostrophe and an -*s*. Explain that you add an apostrophe and an -*s* to nouns to make them possessive. Write *Greg* and *pencil* on chart paper. Ask students how you would show that Greg owns the pen. Add an apostrophe and an -*s*.
- Write the following sentences on chart paper: *The girl's shirt was purple and gray. The girls' locker room has a wet floor.* Ask the students what the difference is between the words *girl's* and *girls'* in the two sentences. Explain that one girl's shirt was purple, so the noun is singular. In this case, you need to add an apostrophe and an -*s* to show possession. Explain that the locker room belongs to many girls, so the noun is plural. It needs an apostrophe after the -*s* to show possession.
- Remind students that they share the classroom. Ask them how they would write *It is the students' classroom.* Write the correct sentence on chart paper. Do the same for *Teachers' cars are parked in the parking lot* and *Many girls' shoes got wet.*
- Explain to students the rules for forming possessives. *A singular possessive is formed by adding an apostrophe and an* -s *to a singular noun. If the noun is plural, the possessive is usually formed by adding an apostrophe after the* -s.

Extending the Lesson

Write the sentences in the margin on the board. Have students suggest the possessive noun form. Then have students rewrite the sentences using these possessive nouns.

On Your Own

Have students look around the classroom to identify objects that belong to a classmate or classmates, such as *Jack's pencil* or *Soon Yi's book.* Ask them to list as many of these items as they can find.

1. My _____ name is Sonia. (mother)

2. My _____ cat is black and white. (cousins)

3. _____ backpack is green. (Maliq)

4. Our _____ bikes are brand new. (neighbors)

Assess Progress

Note whether students are able to follow the rules of possessive nouns. Reinforce understanding as the class reads other material with possessive nouns.

Theme ⑥
Review Nouns

Lesson Background

Students should be able to differentiate between common and proper nouns. They should understand the distinction between singular and plural nouns and be familiar with the conventions for putting nouns in plural form. They should understand what a possessive noun is. They should be able to recognize and distinguish between these various noun categories.

Teaching the Lesson

- To review nouns, read aloud the relevant portions of pages 20–21 of the Writer's Handbook as students follow along.

- Divide the class into five groups. Write these categories on chart paper: *Plural, Singular, Common, Proper*, and *Possessive*. Tell students that each group needs to decide what kind of noun the words you will read aloud are and write down their answers. Remind students that nouns can belong to more than one of these categories. Read the following words: *penguins, Mr. Harris, girls, Grandpa*, and *brother's hat*. Write the nouns on the chart paper. Ask groups to give their answers and explain why they made their choices. Correct answers: *penguins* (common, plural); *Mr. Harris* (proper, singular); *girls* (common, plural); *Grandpa* (proper, singular); *brother's* (common, singular, and possessive); *hat* (common, singular).

- Explain to students the different types of nouns. *If a noun is proper, it names a specific person, place, or thing, and the first letter is capitalized. If it is common, it names a general person, place, thing, or idea, and the first letter is not capitalized. Plural nouns name more than one person, place, thing, or idea. Possessive nouns show ownership.*

Extending the Lesson

Copy the sentences in the margin onto chart paper. Have students write the sentences out, filling in the correct form of the noun in parentheses.

On Your Own

Divide students into pairs. Give each pair a page from a book at their level. Instruct them to identify each noun on the page. Have them first determine whether each noun is singular or plural, then whether it is proper or common, and finally whether it is possessive.

You Will Need

- Writer's Handbook, pages 20–21
- chart paper and marker
- several books for noun identification
- paper; two sheets per group, one sheet per student, and one sheet per pair
- pencils

1. Three ____ ate their apples. (student) [students]
2. That is ____ homework. (Kim) [Kim's]
3. The ____ is in New York. (empire state building) [Empire State Building]
4. ____ dog won first prize. (Jim) [Jim's]
5. The ____ den is dark inside. (lion) [lion's]
6. Two ____ jackets were found. (boys) [boys']

Assess Progress

Note whether students are able to differentiate among forms of nouns. Provide additional practice if necessary.

Action and Linking Verbs

Lesson Background

Students already know verbs as action words. Action verbs show what the subject of a sentence does. Linking verbs connect a subject to a noun or an adjective in the predicate.

Teaching the Lesson

- To review action and linking verbs, read aloud the relevant portions of pages 23–24 of the Writer's Handbook as students follow along.
- Write the following sentence on chart paper: *Pablo walks to school every morning.* Ask students to identify the verb. Underline *walks.* Tell students that the verb *walks* is an action verb because it tells what action Pablo is doing. Then write *Pablo is fast.* Ask students to identify the verb. Underline *is.* Explain that the verb *is* in the second sentence is a linking verb because it links the subject *Pablo* to the adjective *fast.*
- Draw a T-chart on the board. Label one column *Action Verbs* and the other *Linking Verbs.* Tape the index cards next to the chart. Ask students to identify the action verbs and the linking verbs. Have volunteers place the cards in the correct columns. Ask students to explain the difference between the two types of verbs in their own words.
- Explain to students the differences between action verbs and linking verbs. *Action verbs show what a subject is doing. Linking verbs connect a subject to a noun or an adjective in a sentence.*

Extending the Lesson

Write the paragraph in the margin on chart paper and read it aloud. Have students copy the sentences and underline the verbs. Have them identify each verb as an action verb or a linking verb.

On Your Own

Divide students into groups of four. Have each group write a paragraph about getting to school every morning. Ask them to use at least two linking verbs and three action verbs. Then ask one group to read its paragraph aloud to the class. Have other students identify which sentences have action verbs and which have linking verbs.

You Will Need

- Writer's Handbook, pages 23–24
- chart paper and marker
- index cards with the following words written on them: *run, play, drive, catch, eat, was, seem, is, are,* and *am*
- paper and pencils for groups and individual students
- tape

The sun <u>was</u> warm. (linking) The birds in the trees <u>chirped</u> and <u>sang</u>. (action, action) Eric <u>waved</u> hello to his friends. (action) They <u>sat</u> down next to him in class. (action) Eric <u>was</u> ready for school to begin. (linking)

Assess Progress

Note whether students are able to differentiate between action verbs and linking verbs. Provide additional practice if necessary.

Main and Helping Verbs

Lesson Background

A sentence can have more than one verb. The most important verb in the sentence is the main verb. It shows the action. Helping verbs come before the main verb of a sentence. They often help create tenses.

Teaching the Lesson

- To review main and helping verbs, read aloud the relevant portions of pages 23–24 of the Writer's Handbook as students follow along.
- Write the following sentence on chart paper: *Sofia will run the race tomorrow.* Ask students to identify the main verb in the sentence. Explain that *run* is the main verb because it shows the action. Now have students identify the verb before the main verb. Explain that *will* is the helping verb because it changes the tense, or when the action happens.
- Write the following sentence on chart paper: *The dog has eaten his food.* Ask a volunteer to decide which is the helping verb and which is the main verb. (*has* = helping, *eaten* = main) Label the verbs. Ask students to explain how the helping verb changes the main verb. Guide students toward explaining that helping verbs show time. Repeat with *Mrs. Tate will call you* and *Ron did talk to Jenna.*
- Explain to students the difference between main and helping verbs. *Main verbs show action. Helping verbs come before main verbs. They help show the time when the main verb's action occurs.*

Extending the Lesson

Tape a sentence strip to the board. Ask students to identify the main and helping verbs in the sentence. Underline the helping verb and circle the main verb. Ask students to explain what the helping verb does to the sentence (*e.g.*, makes it happen in the future). Repeat with the remaining sentence strips.

On Your Own

Write the paragraph in the margin on chart paper. Have students copy the paragraph and identify the main verbs and circle them. Then instruct students to identify the helping verbs and underline them.

You Will Need

- Writer's Handbook, pages 23–24
- chart paper and marker
- sentence strips with the following sentences written on them:
  Ned will eat an apple.
  Gin has cleaned his room.
  Latoya will not sing in the concert.
  Lupe is walking to school.
  Dave was writing a letter.
  Eva did clap at the end of the song.
- paper and pencils for groups and individual students
- tape

Sofia has <u>trained</u> hard for the race. She <u>will</u> (run) many miles in the marathon. She has been (running) every day. She <u>will</u> (run) fast during the race.

Assess Progress

Note whether students understand main verbs and helping verbs. Provide additional practice if necessary.

Past, Present, and Future Verb Tense

Lesson Background

A verb can show an action that happened in the past, is happening in the present, or will happen in the future. The aspect of verbs that shows time is called verb tense. Tense is shown by suffixes, helping verbs, or both. Students must use tense to set their writing in a specific time.

Teaching the Lesson

- To review past, present, and future verb tenses, read aloud the relevant portion of page 26 of the Writer's Handbook as students follow along.
- Write these sentences on chart paper: *Diego works hard on his science project. He worked on it last night. Diego will work on it tomorrow morning.* Ask students to explain the differences between the verbs in the three sentences. Circle *works*, *worked*, and *will work*.
- Draw the four-column chart in the margin on chart paper. Have students form verbs in each tense: past, present, and future.
- Read three sentences from books, one each in past, present, and future tense. Ask students to identify when the action is taking place. Then have students state the tense of each verb.
- Explain to students how to form verb tenses. *Verb tenses show when an action takes place. You can change the tense of verbs by adding different endings and helping verbs.*

Extending the Lesson

Tell students they will compose three paragraphs about travel, which you will record on chart paper. Say *Yesterday we woke up in Hawaii. Tell me what we did, ate, wore, and saw.* Write the four response sentences on the chart. Ask students to identify the verbs and their tense (past). Direct students to now pretend that the class will be going to Hawaii tomorrow. *How will the paragraph change to reflect the future tense?* Make these verb changes to the paragraph and read the new one aloud. Follow the same steps to conclude with a third paragraph set in the present tense.

On Your Own

Draw the three-column chart in the margin on chart paper for students to copy. Have students write one present tense sentence in the chart. Have them rewrite the sentence in each tense. Then tell students to fill in the verb column.

You Will Need

- Writer's Handbook, page 26
- chart paper and marker
- paper and pencils for students
- books for verb tense examples

Verb	Past	Present	Future
play			
climb			
plant			
talk			
work			

Tense	Sentence	Verb
present		
past		
future		

Assess Progress

Note whether students are able to form past, present, and future tense. Provide additional practice if necessary.

Theme 8

Irregular Verbs

Lesson Background

An irregular verb is a verb that has nonstandard conjugation. When forming the past tense form of an irregular verb, an ending of -*ed* is not added. Instead, students must learn the past tense forms of these verbs.

Teaching the Lesson

- To review irregular verbs, read aloud the relevant portion of page 25 of the Writer's Handbook as students follow along. From the list of present and past tense verbs, choose two or three words that your students use every day (*e.g., get/got, know/knew, eat/ate*). Then give examples of past and present verb forms in sentences for each of your chosen verbs.
- Write the following sentence on chart paper: *Melinda draws a picture of her dog.* Ask students to change the sentence into the past tense. Then write this new sentence on the chart paper. Ask students to tell you the difference they see between the verbs.
- Draw a chart on chart paper like the one shown in the margin. Ask students to come up to the chart paper and write a word to complete the chart.
- Explain to students the proper way to conjugate irregular verbs. *Irregular verbs do not end in -ed when telling a past action. Instead, they have different forms that you must learn.*

Extending the Lesson

Divide students into pairs. Have one student write a sentence using an irregular verb he or she finds listed on page 25 of the Writer's Handbook. Then tell his or her partner to identify which tense is used in the sentence. Have the partner rewrite the verb in a different tense.

On Your Own

Have students look through books you have in the classroom to find irregular verbs. Instruct students to write down four irregular verbs they find. Have them identify the tense of the verb and then write the verb in a different tense.

You Will Need

- Writer's Handbook, page 25
- chart paper and marker
- books for irregular verb examples
- paper and pencils for pairs and individual students

Present Tense	Past Tense
am	
	drew
give	
	fell
	threw
do	

Assess Progress

Note whether students are able to conjugate irregular verbs. Provide additional practice if necessary.

Review Verbs

Lesson Background

Verbs are words that show action or connect subjects to other words in sentences. They can be separated into the categories of action and linking verbs. Action verbs show what a subject does. Linking verbs connect a subject to a noun or an adjective in the predicate. Another way that verbs can be categorized is helping verbs versus main verbs. Helping verbs come before the main verb of a sentence. They help to show action and time.

Teaching the Lesson

- To review verbs, read aloud the relevant portions of pages 23–26 of the Writer's Handbook as students follow along.
- Write this sentence on chart paper: *Sofia will ride her bike when she is ready.* Ask students to identify the action verb, helping verb, and linking verb in the sentence. Explain to students that *ride* is the action verb because it tells Sofia's action. *Will* is the helping verb, because it tells when Sofia rides her bike. *Is* is the linking verb, because it connects the subject to another part of the sentence.
- Hold up one sentence strip and ask students to classify the verb or verbs in it. Repeat with the rest of the sentence strips.
- Explain the different types of verbs to students. *Verbs can be categorized as action, linking, and helping verbs. Action verbs show what a subject is doing. Linking verbs connect a subject to words in the predicate. Helping verbs work with the main verb of a sentence to show tense.*

Extending the Lesson

Read aloud the paragraph in the margin. As you read, have students make a list of all the verbs they hear. Have them identify each type of verb. Write the paragraph on chart paper and have volunteers identify and categorize each verb for the class.

On Your Own

Have students look through books you have in the classroom and ask them to find two examples each of action verbs, linking verbs, and helping verbs. Ask students to make a chart with their examples and use the verbs to write their own sentences.

> Lee plays baseball every weekend. He has thrown the ball right past the batters. Last Saturday was sunny and nice for the game.
> [plays = action,
> has = helping,
> thrown = action, main;
> was = linking]

Assess Progress

Note whether students understand the three types of verbs. Provide additional practice if necessary.

Singular and Plural Pronouns

Lesson Background

Pronouns are substitute words for common or proper nouns. Once a noun has been named in a text, a pronoun such as *he*, *she*, or *it* can replace the noun. A pronoun is either singular or plural, depending on the noun it replaces.

Teaching the Lesson

- To review singular and plural pronouns, read aloud the relevant portion of page 22 of the Writer's Handbook as students follow along.
- Read the following two sentences aloud: *David likes to walk his dogs. He walks them every day.* Write the sentences on chart paper. Explain to students that in the second sentence, the word *he* refers to *David*. Since *David* is a singular noun, the singular pronoun *he* replaces it. Tell students that the plural noun *dogs* is replaced by the plural pronoun *them* in the second sentence.
- Draw a T-chart on the board. Label one side *Nouns* and the other side *Pronouns*. Tape the index cards in random order next to the chart. Then ask students to move each noun to the appropriate side of the chart. Then have students tape the corresponding pronoun next to each noun (*e.g.,* *it* next to *pen*).
- Explain to students how to use singular and plural pronouns. *Instead of repeating the same noun over and over, you can replace it with a pronoun. Make sure to replace singular nouns with singular pronouns and plural nouns with plural pronouns.*

Extending the Lesson

Have students use books you have in the classroom to find examples of singular and plural pronouns. Have them write down two singular and two plural pronouns and the nouns that they replace. Ask two volunteers to share their lists with the class.

On Your Own

Divide students into pairs. Have each pair write a paragraph about visiting a friend. Tell them to use at least two singular pronouns and two plural pronouns in their paragraphs.

Nouns	Pronouns
Sonia	she
pen	it
Darnell	he
Sammy and Kay	they

Assess Progress

Note whether students are able to construct sentences with singular and plural pronouns. Provide additional practice if necessary.

Subject and Object Pronouns

Lesson Background

A pronoun is a word that replaces a noun. A subject pronoun replaces the subject of a sentence. An object pronoun replaces the direct or indirect object in a sentence. Subject pronouns include *I, you, he, she, it, we,* and *they.* Object pronouns include *me, you, him, her, it, us,* and *them.*

Teaching the Lesson

- To review subject and object pronouns, read aloud the relevant portion of page 22 of the Writer's Handbook as students follow along.
- Read the following sentence aloud: *They sang a beautiful song to me.* Write the sentence on chart paper. Have students identify the two pronouns in the sentence. Explain that *they* is the subject pronoun because it is the subject of the sentence. Explain that *me* is the object pronoun because it is used after an action verb.
- Draw a T-chart on chart paper. Label the left column *Subject Pronouns* and the right column *Object Pronouns.* Hold up a sentence strip. Ask students to identify the pronouns in the sentence. Ask which is in the subject of the sentence. Write that pronoun under *Subject Pronouns.* Ask which pronoun is used after the verb. Write that pronoun under *Object Pronouns.* Repeat with the remaining sentence strips.
- Explain to students the difference between subject pronouns and object pronouns. *A subject pronoun, such as* I, you, he, she, it, we, *and* they, *replaces the subject of a sentence. An object pronoun, such as* me, you, him, her, it, us, *and* them, *is used after an action verb in a sentence.*

Extending the Lesson

Write the sentences in the margin on chart paper. Have students copy the sentences and underline the subject pronouns once and object pronouns twice.

On Your Own

Have students look through books or magazines and choose five sentences that contain pronouns. Tell students to copy the sentences onto a sheet of paper. Instruct students to underline all the subject pronouns once and the object pronouns twice in their chosen sentences.

1. <u>We</u> need <u><u>you</u></u> to go to the store.
2. <u>She</u> threw the ball to <u><u>him</u></u>.
3. <u>He</u> drew a nice picture for <u><u>us</u></u>.
4. <u>I</u> saw <u><u>them</u></u> at school.
(single underline = subject pronoun, double underline = object pronoun)

Assess Progress

Note whether students are able to use subject and object pronouns properly. Provide additional practice if necessary.

Contractions

Lesson Background

A contraction is a shortening of words by omission of sounds or letters. An apostrophe takes the place of the missing sounds or letters, and a new word is formed. Although contractions are not usually used in formal writing, such as reports, they are essential when trying to reproduce spoken English.

Teaching the Lesson

- To review contractions, read aloud the relevant portion of page 18 of the Writer's Handbook as students follow along.

- Write the words *can not* and *can't* on chart paper. Ask students to identify the letters that are the same. Then ask them what is different about the words. Circle the apostrophe and explain that *can't* is a contraction for the words *can* and *not*.

- Tape the index cards for the individual letters that spell *can not* to the board. Have students tell you which cards to remove in order to make the contraction *can't*, then where to add the apostrophe. Point out that the apostrophe takes the place of the letters that were removed.

- Show students a page from a work of fiction that has contractions and ask them to find the contractions. Write the contractions they find on the board, and then write the two words that make up each contraction. For example: *don't = do + not*; *wasn't = was + not; I've = I + have*

- Read the sentences from your chosen book that have contractions. Then reread the sentences, saying each contraction as two words.

- Explain to students the proper way to use contractions. *Contractions make writing sound less formal, as when someone is speaking. However, when we write reports, we should make our writing sound more formal. Then it is better not to use contractions.*

Extending the Lesson

Write the paragraph in the margin on chart paper, and read it aloud. Have students identify the words that can be made into contractions. Circle the words and ask students to help you write each pair of circled words as a contraction.

On Your Own

Have students look through other works of fiction you have in class and ask them to find contractions. Tell students to write down five contractions they find. Then ask them to write the words used to form the contractions.

"I can not find my math book," Julio said. "I put it in my bag, but it is not there now. If I do not finish my math homework, I am not going to be able to play soccer this afternoon."

Assess Progress

Note whether students can form contractions. Provide additional practice if necessary.

Adjectives: Comparative and Superlative

Lesson Background

Comparative and superlative adjectives compare people, places, things, or ideas. Using comparative language allows students to develop connections and relationships between ideas and gives them tools to point out differences in nouns.

Teaching the Lesson

- To review comparative and superlative adjectives, read aloud the relevant portion of page 27 of the Writer's Handbook as students follow along.
- Hold up two different-sized triangles. Ask students to compare the triangles. Repeat comparative adjectives they mention, such as *larger*, *smaller*, *longer*, and *taller*. Explain that you use the suffix -*er* to mean *more*.
- Hold up three different-sized triangles. Now ask students to compare all three. If they do not use superlatives in their speech (*biggest*, *tallest*), guide them to do so by asking questions (e.g., *Which is biggest?*). Explain that you use the suffix -*est* to mean *most*.
- Explain to students the proper way to form comparatives and superlatives. *If you are comparing two objects, you can say which has more of a certain quality than the other with the suffix -er. If you are comparing three or more objects, you can say which has the most of a quality with the suffix -est.*

Extending the Lesson

Write the paragraphs in the margin on chart paper. Have students change the underlined words into comparative or superlative forms.

On Your Own

Have students choose any two objects. Tell them to write two sentences to compare the objects using comparative adjectives. Then have them add one more object. Instruct students to write two more sentences to compare all three objects using superlative adjectives.

You Will Need

- Writer's Handbook, page 27
- chart paper and marker
- three construction paper triangles of different sizes and with different angles
- paper and pencils for students

The Big Race

The runners lined up and off they went! Jeff was the <u>most fast</u>, but Talesha was the <u>most strong</u>. Shing Ying was <u>more steady</u> than Jeff and Talesha. Talesha jumped <u>more high</u> over a hurdle than Jeff. Shing Ying ran through a puddle and got the <u>most muddy</u>.

Suddenly they heard cheering! Samir, the <u>most slow</u> boy in the class, won! How? He had practiced and trained <u>most hard</u>! [fastest, strongest, steadier, higher, muddiest, slowest, hardest]

 **Assess Progress**

Note whether students are able to use comparative and superlative adjectives. Reinforce understanding as the class reads other material with comparative and superlative adjectives.

Theme ⑪
Articles

Lesson Background

Articles are the most common adjectives students use in writing. Articles can be specific, as in *the*, or nonspecific, as in *a* and *an*. Students must choose the correct article to convey the message they intend.

Teaching the Lesson

- To review articles, read aloud the Tip on page 26 of the Writer's Handbook as students follow along.
- Read these two sentences aloud:
    1. *Marisol told the secret.*
    2. *Marisol told a secret.*

    Ask students to determine and express the difference between the two secrets. Guide them to the understanding that one is specific, or known, and the other is nonspecific, or general.
- Tell students the difference between *a* and *an*. *A* is used before a consonant, and *an* is used before a vowel. Read aloud the following nouns (*cake, envelope, frog, idea, ostrich*) and have students choose an article, *a* or *an*, to precede each word. Write the correct responses on chart paper.
- Explain to students the proper way to use articles. *An article is used just like an adjective. A and an refer to nonspecific nouns, and the refers to a specific noun.*

Extending the Lesson

Write the paragraph in the margin on chart paper. Have students copy the paragraph and fill in the missing articles.

On Your Own

Give students a page from a book at their level. Have them identify each article on the page and determine whether it is specific or general. Ask students to switch *the* for *a* or *an* and see how the change affects the sentence.

You Will Need

- Writer's Handbook, page 26
- books for article identification
- paper and pencils for students
- chart paper and marker

Carlos shopped at the mall.
He really wanted ____ new
shirt. He was hoping for
____ green shirt because
green was his favorite
color. He found one, but
he didn't like it. ____ shirt
had ____ orange pocket, and
he wanted ____ plain green
shirt. [a, a, The, an, a]

Assess Progress

Note whether students are able to choose the appropriate article in a given circumstance. Provide additional practice if necessary.

Theme 12

Adverbs

Lesson Background

Adverbs describe verbs, adjectives, or other adverbs. Most adverbs tell when, where, or how. This lesson will focus on adverbs that modify verbs.

Teaching the Lesson

- To review adverbs, read aloud the relevant portion of page 27 of the Writer's Handbook as students follow along.
- Tell students to listen for the adverb in the following sentence: *Polly played with the dog carefully.* Write the sentence on chart paper. If students cannot identify the adverb, ask *how* Polly played with the dog. *(carefully)* Repeat with *Polly played with the dog here.* Write the sentence on the chart paper, directly underneath the first sentence. If students cannot identify the adverb, ask *where* Polly played with the dog. *(here)* Repeat with *Polly finally played with the dog.* Write the third sentence directly beneath the others on the chart paper. If students cannot identify the adverb, ask *when* Polly played with the dog. *(finally)* Write the word *How* next to *carefully*, *Where* next to *here*, and *When* next to *finally*. Tell students that adverbs are words that tell us how, where, and when an action happens.
- Tell students that many adverbs are formed by adding *-ly* to an adjective.
- Write the sentences in the margin on chart paper. Ask students to identify the words that describe how, when, or where the action happens. Have volunteers come up and underline the adverbs as they are identified.
- Explain to students the definition of adverbs. *Adverbs describe how, when, or where an action takes place. They are often formed by adding -ly to an adjective.*

Extending the Lesson

Divide the class into pairs. Have each pair brainstorm, writing down as many words that end in *-ly* as they can think of in five minutes. Have each pair use two of the adverbs to write sentences. Ask volunteers to read aloud their sentences.

On Your Own

Have students write three sentences about an activity they enjoy. Students should use at least one adverb per sentence. Then ask students to trade papers and circle the adverbs in their partners' sentences.

Ali ran the race <u>quickly</u>.

Liz sings <u>beautifully</u>.

Henry yelled <u>loudly</u>.

Gin <u>suddenly</u> began to giggle.

I sat <u>there</u> <u>quietly</u>.

Assess Progress

Note whether students can identify adverbs. Provide additional practice if necessary.

Theme (12)

Adverbs: Comparison Forms

Lesson Background

Adverbs describe verbs, adjectives, or other adverbs. Comparative adverbs are formed by adding *-er* to one-syllable adverbs, or by adding the word *more* or *less* before longer adverbs. Superlative adverbs are formed by adding *-est* to one syllable adverbs, or by adding *most* or *least* before longer adverbs.

Teaching the Lesson

- To review adverb forms, read aloud the relevant portions of pages 27–28 of the Writer's Handbook as students follow along.
- Write the following sentence on chart paper: *Amelia ran faster than Sharif.* Ask students to identify the word that compares two things. (*faster*) Point out that *faster* tells how Amelia ran, so it is an adverb. Add that it compares how fast Amelia ran to how fast Sharif ran, so it is a comparative adverb.
- Write the following sentence on chart paper: *David worked harder than Rayna, but Rayna was more careful.* Underline *harder* and *more careful.* Tell students that you add *-er* to one-syllable adverbs to make them compare two actions. Explain that for longer words, you use the helping words *less* or *more* to compare two actions.
- Write the following sentence: *Sally sang the loudest of all three girls, but Lisa sang most beautifully.* Ask how many girls are being compared. Tell students that you add *-est* to one-syllable words to make them adverbs that compare three or more actions. Ask students to identify the adverbs. (*loudest, most beautifully*) Explain that for longer adverbs, you use the helping words *most* or *least* to compare three or more actions.
- Explain to students the correct way to form adverbs. *Comparative adverbs compare two actions. They either end in -er or include the helping words* more *or* less. *Superlative adverbs compare more than two actions and either end in -est or include the helping words* most *or* least.

Extending the Lesson

Write the sentences in the margin on chart paper. Have students fill in the appropriate adverb form. (*highest, louder, most patient, more skillfully*)

On Your Own

Have students copy the chart in the margin and work in pairs to fill in the appropriate endings that form each type of adverb.

You Will Need

- Writer's Handbook, pages 27–28
- chart paper and marker
- paper and pencil for each student

1. Of all the children, Wai Ling jumped ____ . (high)
2. Jen sang loudly, but Felipe sang ____ . (loud)
3. All three boys waited patiently, but Vinh was the ____ . (patient)
4. Anna drew ____ than Kyle. (skillful)

	-ly	-er/ more	-est/ most
quick			
eager			
graceful			
kind			

Assess Progress

Note whether students understand comparative and superlative adverbs. Provide additional practice if necessary.

Prepositions

Lesson Background

A preposition is a word or phrase that shows a relationship between a noun or pronoun and other words in a sentence. The noun that follows a preposition is the object of the preposition.

Teaching the Lesson

- To introduce prepositions, read aloud the relevant portion of page 28 of the Writer's Handbook as students follow along. Choose two or three prepositions from the list. Use them in sentences as examples for the class.
- Use a chair as a reference point. Hold a sheet of paper over the chair and tell students that the paper is *over* the chair. Tell them that *over* is the preposition. Invite volunteers to hold the sheet of paper in other places and have the class identify each preposition used. Explain that all of those prepositions show the relationship of the paper to the chair in space.
- Write the following sentence on chart paper: *The room was quiet during the test.* Ask students to identify the preposition in the sentence and then circle it. Explain that the preposition *during* shows time.
- Write the paragraph in the margin on chart paper. Read it aloud. Have students circle the prepositions. Explain that the object of a preposition is the noun that follows the preposition. Have students identify the object of each preposition. Underline them as they are identified.
- Explain the role of prepositions. *Prepositions show the relationship of one noun or pronoun to another word in a sentence.*

Extending the Lesson

Have students write this sentence on their paper: *The fox ran _____ the log.* Have students fill in five prepositions from the list on page 28 of the Writer's Handbook that work in this sentence. Have volunteers share their complete sentences with the class.

On Your Own

Have students look at the list of common prepositions on page 28 of the Writer's Handbook and choose five prepositions. Have them write a sentence for each preposition they have chosen. Have students trade papers. Students should circle the prepositions and underline the object of each preposition.

You Will Need

- Writer's Handbook, page 28
- sheet of paper and a chair
- chart paper and marker
- paper and pencil for each student

Penny walked (through) the gate (to) the <u>zoo</u>. She walked (by) the <u>lions</u>. She walked (down) a <u>ramp</u>. She stood (outside) the <u>aquarium</u>. Her favorite fish was (behind) the <u>glass</u>. Penny's favorite fish was a shark (with) sharp <u>teeth</u>.

Assess Progress

Note whether students can identify and use prepositions. Provide additional practice if necessary.

Prepositional Phrases

Lesson Background

A preposition shows the relationship between a noun or pronoun and another word in a sentence. A prepositional phrase is made up of a preposition, the object of the preposition, and all the words between them.

Teaching the Lesson

- To introduce prepositional phrases, read aloud the relevant portion of page 28 of the Writer's Handbook as students follow along.
- Tape the word strips on the left side of the board, in random order. Tape the prepositional phrase word strips on the right side of the board, also in random order. Have a volunteer make a sentence by matching up a strip on the left with a strip on the right. Ask students to identify the preposition. Circle it. Ask students to identify the object of the preposition, or the noun that comes after the preposition. Circle it. Explain that a prepositional phrase starts with a preposition, ends with the object of the preposition, and includes all the words in between. Underline the whole prepositional phrase. Repeat with the remaining words strips.
- Define prepositional phrases for students. *A prepositional phrase contains a preposition, the object of the preposition, and everything in between.*

Extending the Lesson

Copy the clauses in the margin onto chart paper. Have volunteers underline the prepositions and circle the objects of the prepositions. Have them underline the full prepositional phrases.

On Your Own

Have each student write three sentences about his or her favorite summer activity. The sentences must include prepositions. Ask students to exchange papers with partners. Have them underline the prepositions, circle the object of each preposition, and highlight the prepositional phrases.

You Will Need

- Writer's Handbook, page 28
- chart paper and marker
- word strips with the following clauses written on them:
  Hippos sink
  Tropical birds sing
  You can see monkeys jump
- word strips with the following prepositional phrases written on them:
  into the muddy ponds.
  behind the tree.
  in the sky.
- paper, highlighter and pencil for each student
- tape

1. In the winter, I will go sledding with friends.
2. At the store, my mother put milk and eggs in our shopping cart.
3. My dog sleeps under the porch in the shade.
4. I read about sharks in a book.

Assess Progress

Note whether students are able to identify prepositional phrases. Provide additional practice if necessary.

Conjunctions: Coordinate

Lesson Background

A conjunction connects words or phrases. Coordinate conjunctions, such as *and, but, or, nor, for, so,* and *yet,* connect two or more words, phrases, or clauses.

Teaching the Lesson

- To introduce coordinate conjunctions, read aloud the relevant portion of page 29 of the Writer's Handbook as students follow along.
- Write the following sentence on chart paper: *Jenny ate a sandwich and an apple for lunch.* Ask students to identify the conjunction, or connecting word, in the sentence and circle it. Explain to students that the coordinate conjunction *and* connects the phrases *a sandwich* and *an apple* in this sentence.
- Tape the index cards near the chart paper. Ask students to pick the correct conjunctions for the blanks in the middle column. (*and, or, but, so*) Ask students to identify the sentence parts that the coordinate conjunctions connect.
- Write the following sentences on chart paper: *Tim likes fish and meat. Pete will eat a snack or drink orange juice. My family goes hiking, but we don't camp.* Ask students to identify the conjunctions and point out what parts of the sentences they are connecting. (*and, fish/meat; or, eat a snack/drink orange juice; but, My family goes hiking/we don't camp*)
- Explain to students the proper use of coordinate conjunctions. *Coordinate conjunctions, like* and, but, or, *and* so, *connect equal parts in a sentence: two or more words, phrases, or sections of sentences.*

Extending the Lesson

Ask each student to write three sentences, each using a different coordinate conjunction (*and, but, or, nor, for, so, yet*). Have students trade papers and circle the conjunctions in their partners' sentences.

On Your Own

Have students look through books you have in class and ask them to write down three sentences they find that have a coordinate conjunction (*and, but, or,* or *so*). Have students circle the coordinate conjunction and underline the two parts of the sentence that the conjunction connects.

You Will Need

- Writer's Handbook, page 29
- chart paper and marker
- Index cards with *and, or, so* and *but* written on them
- tape
- books for examples of coordinate conjunctions
- paper and pencil for each student
- the chart pictured below written on chart paper (without underlining; underlining represents answer key)

Sentence Part	Conj.	Sentence Part
Rosa needs a <u>pencil</u>		<u>paper</u> to do her homework.
James asked to be the <u>lead actor</u>		<u>director</u> in the school play.
Anne <u>asked for a candy bar</u>		<u>did not get one.</u>
Rhonda is a cheerleader		<u>she had to go to the game.</u>

Assess Progress

Note whether students are able to use coordinate conjunctions correctly. Provide additional practice if necessary.

Conjunctions: Correlative

Lesson Background

A conjunction connects words or phrases. Correlative conjunctions connect equal parts of sentences. A correlative conjunction is always made up of two parts: one precedes the words, phrases, or clauses being connected, and the other connects the words, phrases, or clauses.

Teaching the Lesson

- To introduce correlative conjunctions, read aloud the relevant portion of page 29 of the Writer's Handbook as students follow along.
- Write the following sentence on chart paper: *Winning first place made me feel both proud and happy.* Ask students to identify the correlative conjunctions. Explain that *both* and *and* are used as a pair to connect the adjectives *proud* and *happy.* Repeat with the following sentence: *Neither my aunt nor my uncle likes oranges.*
- Tape the index cards to chart paper. Have students create a sentence about their favorite movie or television character using one of the correlative conjunction pairs on the index cards. Have a few volunteers write their sentences on chart paper. Then ask other students to identify the correlative conjunctions and the parts of the sentences they connect.
- Explain to students the correct way to use correlative conjunctions. *Correlative conjunctions connect two parts of a sentence. They are used in pairs. The most common correlative conjunctions are* either/or, neither/nor, both/and, not only/but, not only/also, *and* whether/or.

Extending the Lesson

Ask students to write three sentences about choosing a pet. Tell them to use at least two of the conjunction pairs taped to the chart paper.

On Your Own

Have students share the sentences they wrote with a partner. Ask students to circle the correlative conjunctions in their partners' work and underline the items they connect.

You Will Need

- Writer's Handbook, page 29
- chart paper and marker
- index cards with *either/or, neither/nor, both/and, not only/but, not only/also,* and *whether/or* written on them
- paper and pencil for each student
- tape

Assess Progress

Note whether students are able to use correlative conjunctions correctly. Provide additional practice if necessary.

Conjunctions: Subordinate

Lesson Background

A conjunction joins words or groups of words. A subordinate conjunction connects a subordinate clause to a main clause. Subordinate conjunctions usually come before subordinate clauses.

Teaching the Lesson

- To introduce subordinate conjunctions, read aloud the relevant portion of page 29 of the Writer's Handbook as students follow along.

- Write the following sentences on chart paper. *I wore a sweater, and it was cold. I wore a sweater because it was cold.* Ask students to find the conjunctions in the sentences. Circle *and* and *because*. Ask students how the meaning of the second sentence is different from the first. (It tells why the person wore a sweater.) Point out that the word *because* changes how *I wore a sweater* and *it was cold* connect to each other. The two parts are not equal like they are with the word *and*. Explain to students that the kind of conjunction that makes the sentence parts unequal is called a subordinate conjunction.

- Write the following sentences on chart paper: *I read a chapter of my book, and I went to bed. I read a chapter of my book before I went to bed.* Ask students which sentence has unequal parts. Tell students that in the second sentence *I read a chapter of my book* is more important than *I went to bed.* Since *before* connects the unequal parts, it is a subordinate conjunction.

- Explain to students the purpose of subordinate conjunctions. *Subordinate conjunctions connect two unequal parts of sentences. Common subordinate conjunctions include the words* because, although, before, *and* when.

Extending the Lesson

Tape the index cards with subordinate conjunctions to the board. Tape a sentence strip below the index cards. Have students choose a subordinate conjunction to fill in the blank. Repeat with the remaining sentence strips. Some sentences have more than one possible answer.

On Your Own

Have students write four sentences, each using one of the subordinate conjunctions listed on the index cards. Have students trade papers and check one another's work.

You Will Need

- Writer's Handbook, page 29
- chart paper and marker
- tape
- index cards with the following words written on them: *because, although, before,* and *when*
- sentence strips with the following written on them:
  ____ *the children rushed around, they didn't bump into one another or get hurt.*
  ____ *Pierre won first prize, he jumped up and down.*
  ____ *Leann goes to bed, she always brushes her teeth and reads a story.*
  Carla likes going to the doctor ____ *he gives her stickers.*
- paper and pencil for each student

Assess Progress

Note whether students are able to use subordinate conjunctions correctly. Provide additional practice if necessary.

Theme (15)

Independent and Dependent Clauses

Lesson Background

An independent clause contains a subject and a verb. It expresses a complete idea and can be a sentence on its own. A dependent clause contains a subject and a verb, but it does not express a complete thought. It cannot be a sentence on its own.

Teaching the Lesson

- To introduce independent and dependent clauses, read aloud the relevant portion of page 36 of the Writer's Handbook as students follow along.
- Write the following sentence on chart paper and read it aloud: *My parents cover their ears when I play the drums.* Explain to students that the first part of the sentence (*My parents cover their ears*) is an independent clause because it can be a sentence by itself. Tell them that the second part of the sentence (*when I play the drums*) is a dependent clause because it is not a sentence by itself.
- Tape the following word strip to chart paper: *Although I am taking swimming lessons.* Ask students if this is a sentence. (no) Tape the word strip *I haven't learned the backstroke yet.* on top of the first strip, covering it. Ask students if this is a sentence. (yes) Move the second word strip so that the two strips are side-by-side and form a sentence. Say *The first part is called a dependent clause because it is the part of the sentence that depends on the other part. The second part is called an independent clause because it can stand on its own as a sentence.*
- Repeat with the remaining word strips.
- Explain to students the difference between independent and dependent clauses. *An independent clause makes sense as a sentence on its own. A dependent clause is not a complete thought and cannot stand alone as a sentence.*

Extending the Lesson

Write the sentences in the margin on chart paper. Ask students to find the independent clauses and circle them. Then have students underline the dependent clauses.

On Your Own

Have students use books you have in class to find two sentences that each contain both an independent and a dependent clause. Instruct students to copy the sentences onto a piece of paper. Ask them to circle the independent clauses and underline the dependent clauses.

You Will Need

- Writer's Handbook, page 36
- chart paper and marker
- books for examples
- strips of paper with the following clauses written on them:
  Although I am taking swimming lessons.
  I haven't learned the backstroke yet.
  Because Keisha likes fruit, her mom puts an apple in her lunch every day.
  Diego goes to the middle school since he is a sixth grader.
- paper and pencil for each student
- tape

1. After I walk the dog, I have to clean my room.
2. We brought a bottle of water so that we wouldn't get thirsty.
3. He likes the car since it's bright red.
4. We brought lunch in case we get hungry.

 **Assess Progress**

Note whether students are able to identify independent and dependent clauses. Provide additional practice if necessary.

Theme ⑯
Homophones

Lesson Background

Homophones are words that sound the same but have different spellings and meanings. Some examples of common homophones are *to/two/too*, *flower/flour*, and *wear/where*.

Teaching the Lesson

- To introduce homophones, read aloud the relevant portions of pages 31 and 50–54 of the Writer's Handbook as students follow along.
- Write the following sentence on chart paper and read it aloud to students: *I don't know whether the weather is nice today.* Ask them which two words sound the same. Explain that the words *whether* and *weather* are homophones because they sound exactly the same, but they are spelled differently and mean different things.
- Write the following sentences on chart paper: *Where will I wear my new dress? (where, wear) Two days ago, I was too sick to come to school. (two, too, to)* Read the sentences aloud. Ask students to identify each homophone. Then have students define them.
- Explain homophones to students. *Homophones are words that sound the same as each other but are spelled differently and mean different things.*

Extending the Lesson

Write the sentences from the margin on chart paper. Have students copy the sentences, writing the correct word in the blank.

On Your Own

Write the following homophone pairs on chart paper: *by/buy, close/clothes,* and *hour/our*. Divide the class into groups of four. Have each group write three sentences containing the homophone pairs listed above.

You Will Need

- Writer's Handbook, pages 31, 50–54
- chart paper and marker
- paper and pencil for each student

1. There is a ____ on the boat. (sale/sail)

2. Do you know when our homework is ____? (do/due)

3. What day of the ____ do you have dance lessons? (weak/week)

4. I liked the last ____ of the play. (scene/seen)

Assess Progress

Note whether students use the correct homophones. Provide additional practice if necessary.

Review Homophones

Lesson Background

Homophones are words that sound the same but have different spellings and meanings. Some examples of homophones are *weather/whether*, *hare/hair*, and *rain/reign*.

Teaching the Lesson

- To review homophones, read aloud the relevant portions of pages 31 and 50–54 of the Writer's Handbook as students follow along.
- Write the following sentence on the board and read it aloud to students: *I want to buy two books, too.* Explain that the words *to*, *two*, and *too* sound exactly the same. They are homophones. Point out that they are spelled differently and mean different things.
- Write the words *pear* and *pair* on chart paper. Ask students to use each word in a sentence. As you write each sentence, ask students how to spell the homophone. Repeat with *right* and *write*.
- Explain to students what homophones are. *Homophones are words that sound the same as other words. However, they are spelled differently and mean different things.*

Extending the Lesson

Write the sentences from the margin on chart paper. Ask students to write the correct homophones in the blanks.

On Your Own

Write the following homophone pairs on chart paper: *know/no*, *its/it's*, and *do/due*. Have students write three sentences about life at school. Have them include and circle all three homophone pairs listed above.

You Will Need

- Writer's Handbook, pages 31, 50–54
- chart paper and marker
- paper and pencil for each student

---

1. He ____ his horse down the ____ . (road/rode)
2. Did you ____ anything out on the ____ ? (see/sea)
3. ____ putting ____ books over ____ . (their/there/they're)
4. He is ____ because his chess ____ is missing. (bored/board)

 **Assess Progress**

Note whether students use the correct homophones. Provide additional practice if necessary.

Name_____ Date _____

Main Idea Organizer

Supporting Detail

Supporting Detail

MAIN IDEA

Supporting Detail

Supporting Detail

Name_____ Date _____

Story Organizer

Title
_____

Setting
_____

_____

Characters
_____

_____

Problem
_____

_____

Events

1. _____

2. _____

3. _____

Solution
_____

Ending
_____

Report Organizer

Main Idea
_____

Supporting Detail

_____

_____

_____

Supporting Detail

_____

_____

_____

Supporting Detail

_____

_____

_____

Conclusion

_____

_____

Name_____ Date_____

Sequence Organizer

Step 1	**Step 2**

Step 3	**Step 4**

Step 5

Sequence Organizer

Name _____ Date _____

Personal Narrative Organizer

Main Idea

_____

Event 1	Feelings
	_____
	_____
_____	_____

Event 2	Feelings
	_____
	_____
_____	_____

Event 3	Feelings
	_____
	_____
_____	_____

Conclusion

_____

_____

Name_____ Date_____

Problem and Solution Organizer

Setting: _____

Characters: _____

Problem	Solution

Problem	Solution

Problem	Solution

Name_____ Date _____

Sequence Organizer

Step 1

Step 2

Step 3

Step 4

Step 5

Name_____ Date_____

Story Organizer

Title
_____

Setting

_____

_____

Characters

_____

_____

Problem

_____

_____

Events

1. _____

2. _____

3. _____

Solution
_____

Ending
_____

Story Organizer

Name_____ Date _____

Biography Organizer

Person: _____

Key Life Events

Name_____ Date _____

Problem and Solution Organizer

Characters

Setting

Problem

Events

Solution

Problem and Solution Organizer

Name_____ Date _____

Persuasive Essay Organizer

What I Think

_____

_____

Reason 1

_____

_____

_____

Reason 2

_____

_____

_____

Reason 3

_____

_____

_____

Conclusion

_____

_____

Letter Organizer

Date

[ ]

Person's Name with Business

[ ]

Salutation

[ ]

Body

[ ]

Closing

[ ]

Letter Organizer

Name_____ Date _____

Cause and Effect Organizer

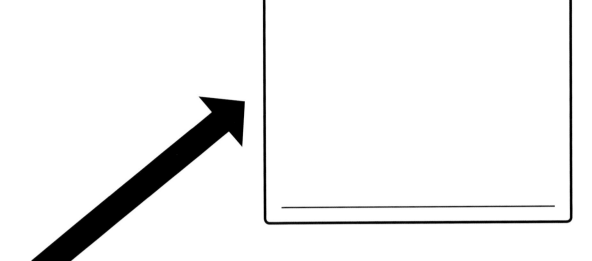

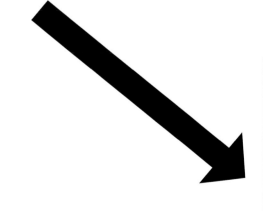

Poem Organizer

Image	Descriptive Words
	_____ _____ _____ _____ _____
	_____ _____ _____ _____ _____
	_____ _____ _____ _____ _____

Name_____ Date_____

Newspaper Article Organizer

Title: _____

Who?	_____ _____ _____

What?	_____ _____ _____

When?	_____ _____ _____

Where?	_____ _____ _____

Why?	_____ _____ _____

Compare and Contrast Organizer

_____ _____

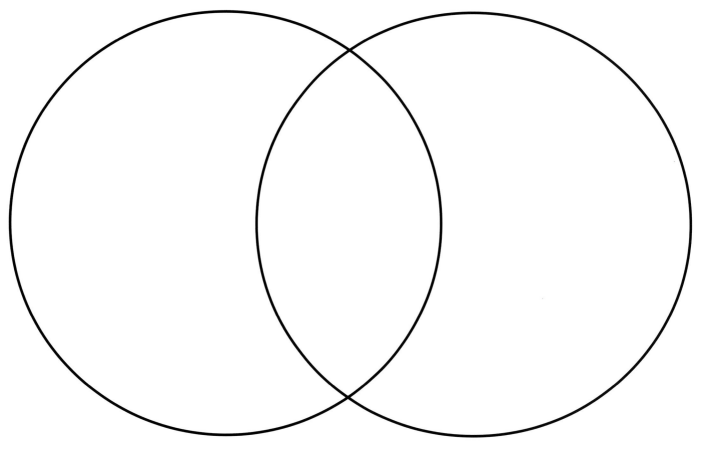

Compare and Contrast Organizer

Start Strong

Engage Your Reader with a Lively Beginning

Lesson Background

An engaging opener is critical to drawing readers into a piece of writing. There are many different ways writers can craft a lively opener. They can begin by describing a scene in detail, by presenting the big picture about a topic, by using sensory language, or by asking an intriguing question. This lesson focuses on the strategy of starting strong by asking a question.

Teaching the Lesson

- Copy and distribute the Start Strong Master on page 50 of this guide. You may wish to make a transparency of this page for use during whole-class instruction.
- Read the selection "The Giant Panda" aloud as students follow along.
- After reading, discuss the selection with students. *What was good about this piece of writing?* (its organization, the information provided) *What needed some improvement?* (the opening) *As a reader, were you very excited to read the rest of the selection after reading the first sentence? Why or why not?* (No, the opening was dull.)
- Tell students that a lively beginning is very important to draw readers into your writing. One way to "grab" the reader at the beginning of a piece of writing is to begin with a question. With students, brainstorm possible questions to serve as an engaging opening sentence to "The Giant Panda." You may wish to suggest the following: *What animal eats bamboo and lives in the bamboo forests of China? What do you know about giant pandas?*
- Have students edit "The Giant Panda" to include a lively opener. They may either record a class suggestion or write a new question of their own.

Extending the Lesson

During small-group writing instruction, have students select a recent piece of writing from their writing folders that they think needs a more engaging beginning. Support students as they revise their writing. Then compare the original and revised versions as a group.

On Your Own

Have students look through other fiction and nonfiction texts to find openers that really engage the reader. Encourage students to record some of these examples in their Writer's Notebook as a source of opener ideas for their own writing.

Assess Progress

Note whether students are able to craft a lively beginning by opening with a question. Provide additional practice if necessary.

The Giant Panda

Giant pandas are very interesting animals. They live in the bamboo forests of China. Giant pandas have to spend most of the day eating. They do this because bamboo, their main food, is a grass. Grasses don't have a lot of vitamins or calories, so bamboo doesn't give pandas much energy. Giant pandas have to eat about fifty pounds of their favorite food every day to survive.

Start Strong!

Write a new opening sentence for "The Giant Panda" by asking a question.

_____

_____

_____

_____

Make Your Ideas Clear

Lesson Background

When writing paragraphs, it is important to make sure the ideas are clear and well-developed. Students can do this by deciding on a main idea, writing a topic sentence, using supporting details, and tying the content together. This lesson focuses on tying supporting details together to form strong paragraphs.

Teaching the Lesson

- Copy and distribute the Build Strong Paragraphs Master on page 52 of this guide. You may wish to make a transparency of this page for use during whole-class instruction.
- Read the selection "The Great Wall" aloud as students follow along.
- After reading, discuss the selection with students. *What was good about this writing?* (It had a good introduction, a clear topic, and supporting details.) *What did you think needed some improvement?* (It had extra and unrelated sentences in it.) *As a reader, were you confused by some of the details in the paragraph? Why or why not?* (Yes, because they didn't tie in to the rest of the paragraph.)
- Tell students that it is important to make sure all the content in a paragraph is about the main idea. *This makes it easier for the reader to understand what the paragraph is about. One way to tie all your content together is to edit your writing after you are finished.* With students, brainstorm items they should look for when editing their paragraphs for tying content together. You may wish to suggest the following: *Look for sentences that don't fit with the topic. Look for sentences about yourself instead of about the topic. These do not belong in the paragraph.*
- Have students edit "The Great Wall" to make sure the content ties together. They may eliminate unrelated sentences suggested by the class or find other sentences that do not belong in the paragraph.

Extending the Lesson

During small-group writing instruction, have students select a recent piece of writing from their writing folders. Have them read over their work to find paragraphs where they need to tie the content together. Support students as they revise their writing. Then compare the original and revised versions as a group.

On Your Own

Have students look through other fiction and nonfiction texts to find paragraphs that are tied together well. Encourage students to record some of these in their Writer's Notebook as examples of strong paragraphs.

Assess Progress

Note whether students are able to build strong paragraphs by tying content together. Provide additional practice if necessary.

The Great Wall

Did you know that there is a giant wall in China? This wall is known as the Great Wall. It is more than 4,000 miles long and more than 2,000 years old. I would love to visit China. The emperors of China had the wall built to protect China from enemies. It is made mostly of mud bricks. Some houses are made of bricks. The wall is so large that it can be seen from space! Someday, I want to be an astronaut.

Tie Ideas Together

Edit the paragraph so that all the ideas are tied together. Remove any sentences that do not match the main idea of the paragraph. Rewrite the new paragraph on the lines below.

_____

_____

_____

_____

_____

_____

Spice Up Your Story with Conversation

Lesson Background

The way that characters speak is a valuable part of writing. When characters speak in a convincing, believable way, readers can relate to the characters and become more engaged in a story. Writers can listen to natural speech patterns and write speech down in order to craft believable dialogue.

Teaching the Lesson

- Copy and distribute the Incorporate Dialogue Master on page 54 of this guide. You may wish to make a transparency of this page for use during whole-class instruction.
- Read the selection "Whose Book Is It?" aloud as students follow along.
- After reading, discuss the selection with students. *What are the characters talking about?* (a book) *Do they sound like kids you know?* (no) *Why not?* (They don't use contractions. They repeat nouns instead of using pronouns.) *Does the speech seem natural?* (no)
- Tell students that the dialogue in a story is just as important as the setting, characters, and plot. Each character must speak in a way that is believable for that character. Ask students if they think that the characters in the example are fourth graders. With students, brainstorm possible ways to fix the dialogue. You may wish to suggest an alternative first line, such as *"Hey, you've got my book!"*
- Have students edit "Whose Book Is It?" to make the dialogue believable. They may record class suggestions or write new, believable dialogue of their own.

Extending the Lesson

During small-group writing instruction, have students select a recent piece of writing from their writing folders that they think needs editing to make the dialogue more natural and believable. Support students as they revise their writing. Then compare the original and revised versions as a group.

On Your Own

Have students look through other fiction and nonfiction texts to find examples of believable dialogue. Encourage students to record some of these examples in their Writer's Notebook as a source of inspiration for the dialogue of their own characters.

 **Assess Progress**

Note whether students are able to craft believable dialogue. Provide additional practice if necessary.

Whose Book Is It?

"That is my book!" said Blanca.

"No, it is my book," said Joe.

"I know it is my book," said Blanca. "It has a picture of a girl with her arm around a pig on the cover. I own that book."

Joe opened the front cover. "I am sorry. I was wrong. *Blanca* is written inside. It is your book."

Make It Sound Real

Change the dialogue in "Whose Book Is It?" so that it sounds more like actual fourth graders are speaking. Write the new dialogue on the lines below.

_____

_____

_____

_____

_____

_____

Use Active Words and Phrases

Lesson Background

Vivid and original wording is essential for engaging a reader and keeping his or her attention. Students can keep their language fresh by using active verbs, meaningful adjectives, and specific nouns, as well as avoiding the passive voice. This lesson focuses on recognizing empty adjectives and replacing them with more meaningful and specific descriptions.

Teaching the Lesson

- Copy and distribute the Keep Language Fresh Master on page 56 of this guide. You may wish to make a transparency of this page for use during whole-class instruction.
- Read the selection "Mahala's Horrible Day" aloud as students follow along.
- After reading, discuss the selection with students. *Did the description in the story help you understand Mahala's feelings?* (No, it didn't give much information.) *How do you think the writer could improve this piece of writing?* (use more specific description)
- Tell students that adjectives like *good, bad,* and *nice* are so general that they can mean almost anything. *If I tell you that Joey is a good student, you don't know if I mean he follows directions, always does his homework, is kind to his classmates, or gets good grades. Since I'm not giving you any information, my description doesn't mean anything.* Explain that choosing more specific and descriptive wording helps the reader understand and "see" your story.
- Ask students what bad feeling Mahala is having in the first sentence. You may wish to suggest *scared, worried,* or *nervous.*
- Have students circle the empty adjectives in "Mahala's Horrible Day." Ask them to edit the story to include more meaningful description.

Extending the Lesson

During small-group writing instruction, have students select a recent piece of writing from their writing folders that they think needs editing to eliminate empty adjectives. Support students as they revise their writing. Then compare the original and revised versions as a group.

On Your Own

Have students look through other fiction and nonfiction texts to find examples of vivid description. Encourage students to record some of these examples in their Writer's Notebook as a source of inspiration for description in their own stories.

 Assess Progress

Note whether students are able to use language that makes their writing fresh and interesting. Provide additional practice if necessary.

Mahala's Horrible Day

Mahala felt bad. She was going to take a math test the next day. She thought science and reading were good subjects, but math was hard. Then her dad said he would help her study. She thought that was a nice thing to do. It made her feel good. Her little brother Andrew said something nice to Mahala. He said she was a good student and she shouldn't worry about the test.

Keep Language Fresh

Circle the empty adjectives in "Mahala's Horrible Day." Then rewrite the story, replacing those adjectives with more meaningful descriptions.

_____

_____

_____

_____

_____

_____

Create an Atmosphere

Lesson Background

A strong setting transports readers to the location of a story. Writers can create an atmosphere by describing the physical setting, describing the weather, using the five senses, and even showing the impact of the setting on a character. This lesson will focus on using the five senses to bring a setting to life.

Teaching the Lesson

- Copy and distribute the Establish Setting Master on page 58 of this guide. You may wish to make a transparency of this page for use during whole-class instruction.
- Read the selection "House on the Hill" aloud as students follow along.
- After reading, discuss the selection with students. *What was the setting of this story?* (a scary hilltop) *How did the setting make you feel?* (nervous, cold, uncomfortable) *Did the setting have the same effect on the character?* (Yes, he was afraid.) *As a reader, could you imagine the setting in your mind?* (Yes, it was like I was there.) *Could you see it, hear it, and smell it?* (yes)
- Tell students that a strong setting uses all five senses to give readers the feeling that they are really there. Draw a graphic organizer web on the board. Label the center circle Five Senses. Draw five corresponding circles branching off from the center. Label them See, Hear, Smell, Taste, and Touch. Ask students the following question: *What words or descriptions from the story can we put into each of these circles?* Work with students to complete the graphic organizer.
- Have students revise "House on the Hill" to change the setting from scary to happy. Encourage them to use a five senses graphic organizer to help in their writing.

Extending the Lesson

During small-group writing instruction, have students select a recent piece of fiction writing from their writing folders that they think needs a more vivid setting. Support students as they revise their writing. Then compare the original and revised versions as a group.

On Your Own

Have students look through other fiction texts to find strong settings that make the reader feel like he or she is right in the middle of the action. Encourage students to record some of these passages in their Writer's Notebook as examples of establishing setting.

Assess Progress

Note whether students are able to craft a strong setting that uses all five senses. Provide additional practice if necessary.

House on the Hill

A thick curtain of fog rolled over the hilltop. It came from the river below and carried the smells of fish and mud with it. The gray cloud was so thick Jeremy could not see two feet in front of him. However, he could hear crickets chirping. A freezing wind whipped through the holes in Jeremy's sweatshirt, and he shivered.

In front of Jeremy, a big old house stood at the highest point on the hill. It sat close to the cliff's edge, as if ready to jump.

Paint a Picture with Words

Use the five senses to change the setting for "House on the Hill" from scary to happy.

_____

_____

_____

_____

_____

_____

Aim at the Right Target

Lesson Background

Once a student understands the purpose of a piece of writing as well as who is going to read it, he or she can choose topics, details, and examples that will convey the intended meaning in an appropriate way. This lesson focuses on the strategy of choosing appropriate details.

Teaching the Lesson

- Copy and distribute the Adapt to Purpose and Audience Master on page 60 of this guide. You may wish to make a transparency of this page for use during whole-class instruction.
- Read the selection "Vote for Me!" aloud as students follow along.
- After reading, discuss the selection with students. *What is the purpose of this piece of writing?* (to get students to vote for Harry for class president) *Who is it written for?* (Harry's classmates) *As a reader are you persuaded to vote for Harry in the election? Why or why not?* (No, because the details aren't about why he will be a good president. They are aimed at making friends, not getting kids to vote for him.)
- Tell students that it is important to consider details when writing for a particular reason. *Harry should tell everyone how he will make a good president, but he doesn't choose the right details to accomplish this purpose. One way to make sure you include the right details is to think about your purpose.* Ask students what changes they might want a class president to make. You may wish to suggest the following: *Harry could talk about making recess longer or asking for spaghetti to be served at lunch.*
- Have students edit "Vote for Me!" to make it better adapted to its purpose and audience. They may use details suggested by the class or think of their own.

Extending the Lesson

During small-group writing instruction, have students select a recent piece of writing from their writing folders that they think could be better adapted to the purpose and audience. Support students as they revise their writing. Then compare the original and revised versions as a group.

On Your Own

Have students look through other fiction and nonfiction texts for writing that is well adapted to a purpose and an audience. Encourage students to record some of these in their Writer's Notebook as examples of writing that is adapted to a purpose and an audience.

Assess Progress

Note whether students are able to adapt their writing to a purpose and an audience using appropriate details. Provide additional practice if necessary.

Vote for Me!

My name is Harry, and I am running for class president. I will make a great class president. I think I could really make some great changes to the school. I love spaghetti, but I don't like pizza. My favorite color is blue. Autumn is my favorite season. Vote for me, Harry, for your next class president!

Know the Purpose

Find the details that Harry should change. Replace them with details that fit Harry's purpose of getting elected.

_____

_____

_____

_____

_____

_____

_____

Finish on a Strong Note

Lesson Background

The ending of a text is a writer's last chance to make an impression on a reader. Strong endings can help emphasize a point in a persuasive piece of writing or make a creative piece memorable. Strategies for strong endings include asking a meaningful question, using an interesting fact to close a piece, and ending on a humorous note. This lesson will focus on using an interesting fact to close a piece.

Teaching the Lesson

- Copy and distribute the End Effectively Master on page 62 of this guide. You may wish to make a transparency of this page for use during whole-class instruction.
- Read the selection "Big Blue" aloud as students follow along.
- After reading, discuss the selection with students. *What was good about this paragraph?* (It has a lot of amazing facts about blue whales.) *How did the author end this passage?* (with a statement) *Is the last sentence strong? Why or why not?* (No, because it is boring and doesn't tell us any information.)
- Tell students that an effective ending leaves the reader wanting to know more about the topic. One way to keep a reader interested is to finish the paragraph with a strong sentence that tells the reader something interesting.
- Tell students three facts they might wish to incorporate into the paragraph. *Blue whale hearts are the size of small cars. Blue whales are larger than the largest dinosaurs were. Blue whales are louder than jet airplanes.* Have each student pick his or her favorite from among the three fascinating blue whale facts.
- Have students write a new last sentence for "Big Blue" that includes their favorite fascinating blue whale fact.

Extending the Lesson

During small-group writing instruction, have students select a recent piece of writing from their writing folders that they think needs a more effective ending. Have students write two or three endings and then decide on the best one. Then compare the original and revised versions as a group.

On Your Own

Have students look through other fiction and nonfiction texts to find strong endings that keep the reader wanting more. Encourage students to record some of these in their Writer's Notebook as examples of ways to end their writing effectively.

 **Assess Progress**

Note whether students are able to craft effective endings. Provide additional practice if necessary.

Big Blue

There is nothing small about the blue whale. This giant mammal can grow up to 90 feet long and can weigh 150 tons. Blue whales live in the oceans. They eat mainly krill, a shrimp-like animal. Whales eat about 8,000 pounds of krill a day. They live in groups called pods. They are often seen swimming in pairs. They are not only the biggest mammals on Earth, but also the loudest. Blue whales are very interesting mammals.

Tell Us More

Write a new last sentence for "Big Blue" that includes a fascinating fact about blue whales.

_____

_____

_____

_____

Give Your Reader Signposts

Lesson Background

In nonfiction writing, various features help organize the text and provide a roadmap for the reader. Subheadings break up the text and can help the reader find details quickly. Captions give photos and illustrations significance and tie them to the main text. Charts and graphs give a reader visual clues about statistics. This lesson will focus on the use of subheadings.

Teaching the Lesson

- Copy and distribute the Use Nonfiction Features Master on page 64 of this guide. You may wish to make a transparency of this page for use during whole-class instruction.
- Read the selection "Statue Missing from School" aloud as students follow along.
- After reading, discuss the selection with students. *What was good about this piece of writing?* (the information provided, the organization, the suspense about what happened to the statue) *Why do you think the writer included* The Disappearance *and* Town Police Investigate? (to help organize the article)
- Tell students that subheadings can help organize a newspaper article or report. Subheadings break up the text into categories or sections. With students, brainstorm possible subheadings for the third paragraph of "Statue Missing from School." You may wish to suggest the following: *Found with Teacher* or *Now Repaired*.
- Have students edit "Statue Missing from School" to include a third subheading. They may record a class suggestion or write a new subheading of their own.

Extending the Lesson

During small-group writing instruction, have students select a recent piece of nonfiction writing from their writing folders that they think needs subheadings to organize it. Support students as they revise their writing. Then compare the original and revised versions as a group.

On Your Own

Have students look through other nonfiction texts in search of subheadings. Encourage students to record some of these in their Writer's Notebook as examples of subheadings used to organize writing.

 **Assess Progress**

Note whether students are able to craft subheadings to organize nonfiction pieces. Provide additional practice if necessary.

Statue Missing from School

The Disappearance

Students and teachers were shocked Thursday morning. When they arrived at school, they noticed the statue of George Washington was missing.

Town Police Investigate

The principal, Mrs. Green, called the police, who said they would investigate. Officer Ramos called the janitor, Mr. Riley, for information. Mr. Riley said the statue was already gone when he arrived at 6:00 A.M.

_____

The statue was found in Mr. Parks' classroom. Parks said he had removed the statue so he could fix the nose that had broken off. The statue has been repaired and returned to its place by the front door.

Organize Your Writing

Write a subheading for the third paragraph of "Statue Missing from School."

_____

_____

_____

Editing Checklist

☐ My name is on my writing piece.

☐ My writing piece has a title.

☐ I read over my piece twice.

☐ I had a friend edit my piece.

☐ My piece is organized and understandable.

☐ All of the words are spelled correctly.

☐ I capitalized the first letter of each sentence.

☐ I capitalized all proper nouns, including people's names and the word *I*.

☐ Each sentence ends with a period, a question mark, or an exclamation point.

☐ I used quotation marks around sentences where someone is speaking.

☐ My handwriting is neat and clear.

☐ I used apostrophes to show possession.

☐ I checked my grammar.

☐ This is my best work.

Name_____ Date _____

Writer's Reflection Checklist

☐ Title of my writing piece: _____

☐ My favorite part of this piece and why:

_____

_____

_____

☐ What I did to improve my piece was:

_____

_____

☐ What I'm proud of in my writing:

_____

_____

☐ Area I'd like to improve in my writing:

_____

_____

☐ One new idea I have learned about being a writer:

_____

_____

66

Writer's Reflection Checklist

Name_____ Date _____

Writing Traits Checklist

Ideas

☐ I have a clear message or story.

☐ I used important, interesting details to support my writing.

☐ My writing is focused.

Organization

☐ I have a strong beginning and ending.

☐ There is a title on my work.

☐ I put my ideas in an order that makes sense.

☐ I used transition words to create links between ideas.

Voice

☐ My writing expresses my personality and feelings.

☐ My point of view is clear.

☐ I wrote in a style that fits my audience.

Word Choice

☐ I used strong verbs to show action.

☐ I used precise nouns.

☐ I used descriptive words that paint a picture for the reader.

☐ I used exact words.

Sentence Fluency

☐ My writing sounds good when read aloud.

☐ I used connecting words.

☐ I began sentences in different ways.

☐ I varied my sentence length.

Conventions

☐ I checked my spelling.

☐ I used capital letters correctly.

☐ I used punctuation marks correctly.

☐ I checked for verb and pronoun correctness.

☐ I indented my paragraphs.

Presentation

☐ My writing is neat and clear.

☐ I used the correct margins.

☐ I used pictures, charts, or other visuals to add interest.

☐ I added a title.

Name_____ Date _____

Writer's Craft Checklist

☐ My beginning is effective and makes the audience want to continue reading.

☐ My message is clear and aimed at my audience.

☐ I have included enough information and details.

☐ The reader can hear my "voice" in this piece.

☐ I varied my sentence structure.

☐ The sentences in my piece do not all begin with the same word.

☐ I organized my thoughts so my piece is easy to follow.

☐ My piece could easily be read aloud by another person.

☐ I used exciting words that will interest my audience.

☐ I wrote an effective ending.

☐ I edited my piece.

☐ My piece stays on the topic I started with.

Writer's Craft Checklist